Praise for *Tears of Battle*

"One of the first megastars to speak up about the importance of helping animals."

—Ingrid Newkirk, President, PETA

"A critical commentary regarding the justifications for the domination [of animals] in contemporary society."

—*Livres Hebdo*

"The star who gave up her career to fight against abuse . . . a myth and a social phenomenon."

—*Paris Match*

"*Tears of Battle* is a tender adagio of attrition which nevertheless emanates a force that wavers towards the future."

—*Nice-Matin*

"In her new book . . . the icon of French cinema Brigitte Bardot tells of her fight for the animals, who 'saved' her from the dizziness of the limelights, and pleads for 'a common future' for all living things."

—*Agence France Presse*

"A captivating testimony. . . . This book gives a closer look at the life of B.B., not the star adulated, but the other: the lover, the protector of animals, who works tirelessly so that wherever they are on earth, those sentient beings are a little better treated."

—*Tele Star Jeux*

"A fascinating, balanced memoir. . . . These confessions have the force of the upmost frankness."

—*L'Abeille 54*

"She was a sex symbol, a legend, an epic personality . . . [and] a woman of heart, mobilized daily for our animals. And that's not cinema."

—*Midi Libre*

TEARS OF BATTLE

TEARS OF BATTLE

An Animal Rights Memoir

BRIGITTE BARDOT
ANNE-CÉCILE HUPRELLE

Translated by Grace McQuillan

ARCADE PUBLISHING • NEW YORK

First English-language Edition

Originally published in France under the title *Larmes de Combat* by Editions Plon.

Arcade Publishing books may be purchased in bulk at special discounts for sales promotion, corporate gifts, fund-raising, or educational purposes. Special editions can also be created to specifications. For details, contact the Special Sales Department, Arcade Publishing, 307 West 36th Street, 11th Floor, New York, NY 10018 or arcade@skyhorsepublishing.com.

Arcade Publishing® is a registered trademark of Skyhorse Publishing, Inc.®, a Delaware corporation.

Visit our website at www.arcadepub.com.

10 9 8 7 6 5 4 3 2 1

Library of Congress Cataloging-in-Publication Data

Names: Bardot, Brigitte, author.
Title: Tears of battle : an animal rights memoir / Brigitte Bardot, Anne-C?ecile Huprelle ; translated by Grace McQuillan.
Other titles: Larmes de combat. English
Description: First English-language edition. | New York : Arcade Publishing, [2018]
Identifiers: LCCN 2018057097 (print) | LCCN 2018060451 (ebook) | ISBN 9781948924030 (ebook) | ISBN 9781948924023 (hardcover : alk. paper)
Subjects: LCSH: Bardot, Brigitte. | Animal rights activists—France—Biography. | Motion picture actors and actresses—France—Biography. | Animal rights.
Classification: LCC HV4716.B37 (ebook) | LCC HV4716.B37 A3 2018 (print) | DDC 179/.3092 [B]—dc23
LC record available at https://lccn.loc.gov/2018057097

Jacket design by Brian Peterson.
Jacket photograph courtesy of Marc de Raemy

Printed in the United States of America

I dedicate this book to all of the animals who have shared my life and to all of those who share it still.

*"To begin, we will do the
small and simple things; little by little, we will
take on the larger ones, and when the great tasks
are completed, we will set about doing the impossible things."*

—Saint Francis of Assisi
Lover of human and
animal creation

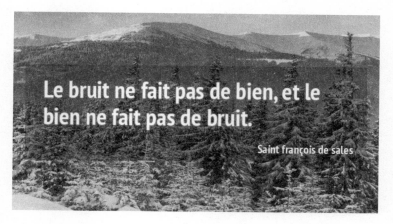

Le bruit ne fait pas de bien, et le
bien ne fait pas de bruit.

Saint françois de sales

"Noise is not good, and the good doesn't make noise."

—Saint Francis de Sales

Contents

Preface

My American friends,

I am immensely grateful to you. Many years ago, when my movie *And God Created Woman* was released in America, it became an instant success, turning me into a worldwide celebrity.

I've used that celebrity to fight for the protection of all animal life for forty-six years now, ever since I understood the extent to which man's cruelty preys on the weakness of other creatures.

My celebrity often brought me close to animals, and I ended up becoming one with them.

I've known the treachery, perversity, faithlessness, ingratitude, and cowardice that man is capable of. I've hated humanity's penchant for destruction and became animal in order not to belong to the inhuman cohort that made me so ashamed.

When I did, I discovered what you will read in this book, the unspeakable suffering that animals are subjected to by man's barbarism every day.

I've been a vegetarian for forty years now. I'm eighty-four years old and super healthy.

My life is forever linked to that of animals, which I consider to be exemplary.

Human dominance has become a barbaric dictatorship over the entire planet, destroying and polluting everything in its wake.

And now, as always, I'm determined to do something about it.

In this book, with the tears of my lifelong battle—my only weapon—I hope to open everyone's heart to compassion, equality among species, antispeciesism, a truly humane way of seeing, and above all the love shared equally among the animals and mankind.

Brigitte Bardot
Saint-Tropez, November 2018

Introduction

"The Blue Hour"

"The Blue Hour" is a unique instant in which the day is giving itself over to the night, and at the same time, the night still belongs to the day. During these fleeting minutes, the day declines and the sky colors itself a dark blue; night has not yet arrived. This period gives rise to displays of rare beauty in nature: flowers exhale their perfumes like never before, and birds sing in chorus before settling down. This interval of time is so marvelously ephemeral that one may wait an entire day to get a taste of its essence when evening comes.

For it is a time outside of time.

The Blue Hour is nature stirring, the animal rejoicing; it is truth without light. And once we have held it, everything is illuminated.

To live the Blue Hour is to hold the instant that flees.

The seven months of work necessary for the realization of this book were permeated with Blue Hours like these, thanks to Brigitte.

In part because she wears "nothing but *L'heure bleue,* that little Essence de Guerlain in her hair," of course, and because her fragrance is so powerful, seductive, and nostalgic, but also because Brigitte understood what I was hoping for.

I approached her the way one approaches a wild animal. With curiosity, gentleness, and patience. At times a lioness, at other times a doe, Brigitte does not allow herself to be easily pinned down. The authenticity of her actions, the reasons for her rebellion, her work with her foundation, and how to make sure that all of these things endure were what had to be at the heart of the text.

So I suggested that she write a book about the meaning of her battle, about her life alongside animals, and about what she wanted to leave behind. I spoke to her about her soul and her animal nature, and about legacy, a word she abhors more than anything. Brigitte agreed without hesitation. I also offered to hold her pen—which in the past she has always refused—and she accepted.

Brigitte's intuition is infallible; she understood where I wanted to go and about the importance of testimony, for both the past and the future. And between those two things is her solitary, simple, and quiet present. I offered her my words, my topics, and my understanding of her existence. The animal battle was at the core of our exchanges, but sometimes memories or anecdotes from her glorious past would insert themselves in a way that made it obvious that this battle had started well before her departure from film: her need to be involved with animals was something she had always carried.

Every Sunday afternoon, we would get together to talk and spend a long and peaceful moment together, the kind that had never been offered to her before and that she had always carefully avoided, probably out of fear of becoming bored. Yes, in addition to being an animal, Brigitte also has the soul of a child: she gets bored very quickly! We conversed and thought together; we breathed and kept quiet.

By listening to Brigitte's breaths and silences, I found that I knew her best.

What interested me in our lengthy discussions was the underside of Brigitte Bardot's image. At one time prisoner of her appearance, she is now prisoner of her impulsivity. I remained faithful to what was interior, underground, to Brigitte's foundations. I wanted to go beyond the sound bites, the controversies, and the pigeonholing interviews, none of which bears any resemblance to the loose and intimate timing of the lady she has become. Where was this animality born, and where did Brigitte's humanity originate? This is the tightrope we walked together that allowed me to understand the peace she was looking for in her moments of introversion, modesty, and wisdom.

This is why, at times, you will not recognize Brigitte Bardot in these lines. Because they belong to our Blue Hours, to those unique, brief, and profound instants where I felt I had truly touched her essence. This is why this book was written with four hands. It takes courage to dig inside yourself, to touch your fragile places and embrace your wounds; it requires audacity to take stock of your life and accept the legacy that will remain. And so Brigitte often needed a double, a mirror, or a consolation. I was there. The rapport we maintain with living beings says everything about who we are. And when our work had reached its end, we both felt orphaned by the loss of those uninterrupted moments spent together.

To hold the instant that flees: autumn's spectacle, the period of dormancy, then recreation for the re-creation. To sit in a corner of the large living room at La Madrague observing Brigitte's movements, still just as sensual and ethereal. To see her grace and tell yourself that the actress never stopped being a dancer, that this woman is a wild cat above all else, and that she must be considered as such.

To hold the instant that flees, like Brigitte's unchanged retort—"One changes lovers, never perfumes"—or her disarming sincerity on the subject of a maternal instinct she once was lacking. When she asked me one day if I myself had such an instinct for my own children, I responded that it was not innate, but acquired; that it was a construction, an apprenticeship. This opportunity had never been offered to her. Before I left, she thanked me: "Maybe I wasn't a complete monster, then. . . ."

To hold the instant that flees, the instant that is too intense, too short, too beautiful; to hold that wordless instant and make it into a book. To live the Blue Hour of this tender, melancholy, and wild animal; to leave my own life for a time in order to reveal the best in hers. To put words to her silences, offer it up to nature, and stretch toward the sky.

The Blue Hour is a beginning, the Blue Hour is an end. It is the possibility of a renewal. It is no longer a dawn, but not yet a sunset.

Anne-Cécile Huprelle
Toulon, France, November 7, 2017

TEARS OF BATTLE

1

The Meaning of My Battle

The Meaning of My Life

I am not part of the human species. I do not want to be a part of it. I feel
different, almost abnormal. As long as the animal is considered an inferior species, as long as we inflict all sorts of evils and sufferings upon
him, and as long as we kill him for our own needs, leisure, and pleasure,
I will not be part of this arrogant and bloodthirsty race. I have always, in
fact, felt very estranged from it.

I share very little with most people, and, *a contrario*, an enormous
amount with a few individuals. Only at rare moments in my life have I
found myself on the same wavelength with beings in whom I recognized
the same outrage, a disgust similar to my own. But most of the time, I
don't know where to place myself in this world of success, superficiality,
and competition.

I know I have lived in that superficiality, but it made me very unhappy.
I never adapted to it; it was always an effort for me. I lived a unique exis-
tence, often one filled with celebrities, sometimes one of high society.
But deep down I did not belong. I have never felt as in sync with myself

as I do today, living almost alone at La Madrague. In harmony with nature.

The first part of my life was like a rough draft for my existence; everything that makes up my life today was already there, in mere seed form. During my adolescence and my career on movie sets, I was always drawn to animals, sensitive to their present and their future. For as long as I can remember, I have had this fierce belief that human beings should protect them, not bully them the way they seemed to be doing.

Today, I can say that I made the right choice: I left cinema in 1973 and have dedicated my days and nights to the creation of an organization that would come to the aid of animals. This has enriched me in many ways. I was able to meet singular beings like the Dalai Lama, as well as wise members of the general public. Beings who carry within them a humanism, a beauty, a simplicity, who live in osmosis with nature, and to whom I owe a great deal. I have often been moved by mystical people whose approach went far beyond spirituality. They told me that the world was so marvelous and vast that we must not restrict ourselves to a narrow vision of it.

The second part of my life, as a result of my encounters and my choices, offered me answers to the questions I had been asking myself up to that point. My animal vocation and my quest for wisdom had been concealed all this time. Life could not possibly be as pointless as what I was seeing. On the other hand, I was embodying the very image of frivolity: I was having fun, I was playing, singing, dancing, loving. I was living, but I never neglected how important certain things were. The heart of my life has never been superficial; on the contrary, it was always quite serious. I often appeared to be enjoying myself, when in fact this was not the case.

So, when I made this life choice at the age of thirty-eight, in the spring of 1973, it came as a surprise even for people who knew me. The man who was sharing my life at the time believed, like many others, that it was a momentary whim. I was just being difficult, and a lot of people told me I would change my mind after three days. I would show the people closest to me this core of authenticity that was always within me, but few of them were really able to perceive it; the only ones who could were those who shared my concerns. My friends, lovers, and parents were often not on the same wavelength as I. They thought my ideas were moments of nostalgia that I would eventually get over. I was always attracted to intense individuals whose introversion allowed them to escape the light, even if they were famous, and cultivate a secret garden, a privacy, something apart.

Compassion

Where does my battle come from? Probably from compassion. Probably from this question that never stops turning around in my mind: "WHO am I, WHO are they asking me to be, and WHO do I want to be?" When I was younger, my husband, the filmmaker Roger Vadim, used to tell me what it was like in the slaughterhouses, though I believe he minimized things a great deal to avoid shocking me. He told me that the killing was done in a certain way, that the largest cows didn't die right away, that the pigs often struggled. . . . I was so naive: at the time, I thought that animals were slaughtered with a single blow, one shot from a revolver. I had not yet become aware of the slaughter systems, the throat-slitting, or the slow deaths. Vadim was also the one who opened my eyes to the prison-like conditions in zoos, and as time went on, I had a lot of questions. I was always drawn to animals, and Vadim would tell me stories the way one might to children: that human beings were not offering animals happy lives, that there was abuse. . . . I was so gullible. My husband would toy with me a little. He even told me once that rats lay eggs.

I was later seriously sensitized to the heinous treatment of slaughter-house animals by a friend, Jean-Paul Steiger, who had founded the Club des Jeunes Amis des Animaux. In the early sixties, he worked for a few days in a slaughterhouse, and this immersion had allowed him to witness the unspeakable: despicable killings and acts of extreme cruelty toward living animals and others who lay dying for endless minutes. More than fifty years before the shock campaigns of the L214 organization, Jean-Paul had taken photos of everyday activities in the slaughterhouses with the means available to him. Those pictures horrified me. I decided that I had to do something. The year was 1962. I went on the television show *Cinq colonnes à la une* as a celebrity to denounce animal throat-cutting, a treatment I thought was worthy of the Middle Ages. We were slicing open the throats of calves, sheep, and other animals in a way that let the blood flow slowly, leaving the living creatures in a state of unimaginable pain. I was sick with fear, sick with stage fright. I was not yet involved with any organization. I was an actress, a star; my only qualification was my desire to rebel. Nervous and only twenty-eight years old, I explained to two "killers" the advantages of a loss of consciousness prior to blood-letting, as well as the benefits of using pistols equipped with a spike to pierce the animal's skull. I also mentioned the possibility of death by gassing. Later, I brought the same arguments to the office of the minister of the interior at the time, Roger Frey. I entered the minister's gilded chambers armed with an electric pistol. This was right in the middle of the Organisation armée secrète (OAS) movement,[1] and his security ser-vice believed I was plotting an assassination. My aim, like other animal defenders, was to get a decree passed that would ban killing without first

1 OAS was a short-lived right-wing French dissident paramilitary organization during the Algerian War, carrying out terrorist attacks in an attempt to prevent Algeria's independence from French colonial rule.

ensuring a loss of consciousness. This law would eventually pass in April 1964, specifying that animals must be inert before being bled.

Alas, this victory was short-lived. The vicious rhythm imposed on these killing centers does not allow animals to receive thorough treatment, so today animals are killed every minute in a production line. Their heads are chopped, their hooves are ripped off, and their bellies are opened and eviscerated, all in record time. All of this is done so quickly that the killers don't even have time to breathe and they become unable to make the connection between the work they're doing and the torture they're inflicting on the animals. What is worse, I have been told by members of my foundation who go to slaughterhouses that the pistols used on the cattle are often ineffective, as is the electronarcosis—stunning by an electric current—that is used on sheep. The modern slaughter industry was modeled after the automobile industry, but we are not talking about bodywork or motors here. We're talking about living creatures.

Man, the Little Nobody

I am very sensitive to the idea of transcendence, to what is beyond us. We are part of a whole, and this fact never leaves me. Nature, earth, and space all form a homogenous and coherent body. I don't confine myself to what is down on earth, because even though the universe is also a black hole—a nothingness, an infinity—this does not frighten me. What does frighten me is being a part of the human race. I have often been reproached for scorning humans; in truth, the only ones I look down upon are those who are self-centered, the narrow-minded spirits, the narcissists, and the arrogant. I scorn a human being when he denies who he is and when he refuses to accept where he comes from and the nature from which he is formed.

We humans are little "nobodies" in the immensity of the universe, and I am certain that if we were to remind ourselves of this truth before anything else when we got up in the morning, many disagreements could be avoided. I don't like airplanes and have always avoided taking them. But each time I have found myself in the air, I have been struck by our smallness: seen from above, men are nothing; they are like ants, grains of sand.

It is probably for this reason that I am attracted by the cosmos. We are governed entirely by the stars, the planets, and their satellites. The moon influences the tides and women's menstruation, and full moons sometimes affect our moods and the reactions of certain animals. The sky transmits waves, whether we like it or not. And this universe is not here for no reason: every element of this vastness exerts a force on our earth. Each human birth is determined by the dancing of the heavenly bodies. At the hour of our arrival on Earth, planets pass in the heavens, aligning with one another, or not, and every fifteen minutes, they emit vibrations that will inhabit us forever. All my life, I have believed that astrology and our birth charts correspond to specific things. I'm not talking about the horoscopes we read in the newspaper. I'm talking about a fundamental astrology. In my memoirs, I talk about a gypsy woman who took hold of my father's hands in a bistro and assured him that his name would be famous across the Atlantic and throughout the world.[2] At the time, he thought it meant that Usines Bardot, his manufacturing company, would become wildly successful. Then when I was eleven, Maman requested a birth chart from a hotshot in the field by the name of Raps. He predicted that I would become extremely famous in an artistic field. Since I was doing a lot of dance at that time, Maman believed I would become a principal dancer. Raps added that I would have a very eventful and

2 Brigitte Bardot, *Initiales B.B.*, Grasset, 1995.

somewhat chaotic life. And indeed, my life never was a long and tranquil river.

I was considered one of the biggest stars in the world, and yet I am nothing. This clarity has always dwelled within me. Despite having a status that is outside the norm, I am nothing, and this certainty comes from my experience of life and its fragility. I learned that human vanity had no purpose when I watched over my dying father night and day in 1975. When life left the body of my poor Pilou, who a few months earlier had been so valiant, and such a poet, I knew that it was useless to cling to anything other than pure love.[3]

All those who govern—the decision-makers—are going to die one day. They are going to rot and become dust again. During the short time we spend on Earth, we are constantly trying to forget that we will all die like idiots. Powerful men, like the stars in the firmament, often believe they will live forever. What saved me was the fact that I never understood my fame. Even now, people continue to talk about me, but I don't know why. I am indifferent to the fact that photos of me are published, or that statues of me are still being erected; I would rather have the production of horsemeat outlawed, or a law passed making it illegal to bleed an animal destined for a dinner plate while he is still alive. It's just like the Legion of Honor: I never went looking for it.

Returning to an almost complete anonymity is my dream. I feel like my own prisoner. Most famous people no longer really belong to themselves. And if today I have agreed to talk about myself so intimately, if I have agreed to publish one last book with my name on it, it is because I need to; I need to sweep away any ambiguity concerning my life and my intentions, for the sake of honesty and transparency. I want to reexamine

---

3 Louis "Pilou" Bardot, business executive, was also a poet. The Académie Française awarded him the Fondation Labbé-Vauquelin Prize for his collection *Vers en vrac*, published in 1960.

the purpose of my battle and remind us once again of the animal's rightful place in our world.

Egoism and Narcissism

Knowing that we are nothing and that this life is but a short passage, each person should spend his or her existence improving nature and the fate of human and animal beings. The very act of reproduction is a selfish need if it is done without thinking about the "all" of which we are a part. I would like us to live within our means: to know our resources and adjust our hunger, our habits. Today, we are beginning to reach our limits: nature is dying, pollution is intensifying, spaces on Earth are being exploited to death, and animal species are disappearing. Egocentrism is the destruction of humanity.

Day after day, we are witnessing this calamity, and yet I have the impression that no one is disturbed by this. Or perhaps the awareness is stuck on an individual and isolated level. The daily massacre of the last elephants is leading to the imminent disappearance of these animals: the whole world should be rebelling in order to prevent the annihilation of an entire race. Giraffes, lions, and rhinoceroses are in danger; armies and soldiers should be sent, not to attack, but to save lives. Does animal life count? Ask anyone on the street and they will wholeheartedly say, "Yes." But as long as the majority of people remain still, no one will move. In a way, humanity remains like an animal: it functions as a herd.

Man is fundamentally selfish, and most people do not react to a cause unless it directly affects them: labor strikes, relocations, job losses, problems concerning their daily life. In these specific cases, people take to the streets, but not for the survival of elephants and other animals. I want the public to be indignant, to come out of its comfort zone, its navel-gazing, to think about something other than the gas meter and washing machine at home.

What I rejected the most during my life as an actress was the limelight. That intense focus on my little person ate at me from the inside. Narcissism is contrary to my nature. When I had to go to film premieres, and all of the spotlights were pointed at me, I hated it. Whenever it was time to decide whether or not to go, my manager usually had to give me a kick in the rear. This worship of celebrity—a life perpetually centered around myself—suffocated me. For quite some time, I could not accept this idolatry, the fact that I was known and recognized because of a few films or the new image of the modern woman they were forging. The second part of my life liberated me. My fame could at last be useful for something, my time on earth could ease some animal suffering. Selfishness is cruel. When we no longer pay attention to anyone, how are we supposed to care about the way we behave toward others?

Cruelty

I started seriously worrying about animals at the end of the sixties. I felt there was injustice being done and no one was concerned about it. Using animals was and still is seen as the most effective way for us to feed, amuse, and dress ourselves. Assassinating animals, every day and billions at a time, was therefore considered normal.

Added to this are the acts of gratuitous cruelty toward animals: I have often wondered about the origins of violence, maliciousness, and cruelty. Man is the only predatory species capable of such perversion and cruelty toward other creatures. This violence has only one goal: possess the other, then exploit it or destroy it.

The scenes of cruelty toward animals that are found posted all over the Internet are nothing short of sadism. A sickness. How could a well-adjusted being find joy in torturing a defenseless animal? Well, I happen to be terrified by other forms of cruelty that are even more devious: I am referring to the cruelty that runs rampant in tradition, industry, and the laboratory.

The "tradition" of the bullfight is nothing more than a monstrous spectacle of agony, suffering, death, blood, and pain. Unfortunately, in this case, the banderillas in the bull's shoulders are not the tools of an isolated sadist, but props in a "show," a sordid ritual. The bull, it seems, has the chance to try and survive or else undergo a death that is considered "honorable." The audience delights in this cruelty.

This same kind of accepted cruelty is present in intensive animal farming. Do you know, for example, what is done to certain male chicks? They are crushed alive because they are unable to lay eggs and because they do not possess the same assets as chickens raised for their flesh. Did you know that a pig's tail is cut off and that his teeth are filed down? How about beak trimming? During this procedure, the chicks are mutilated, their beaks cut by a red-hot blade to keep them from eating their own excrement or pecking at the bodies of their dead companions in the massive sheds where thousands of creatures are concentrated.

Additionally, what takes place in animal experimentation laboratories would make even the most fearsome serial killer tremble: the cruelties inflicted on dogs, cats, monkeys, and rodents go beyond anything we could possibly imagine. If you want to tell me this is a "necessary cruelty," I will prove this is not the case in the chapter dedicated to animal experimentation.

When a person begins to care about animal well-being, I can assure you that he or she will have to endure many sleepless nights. Images circulate in our minds, as do sounds. I have lived many moments of terror—and tears, of course—with this question on my heart: apart from the people giving orders, who are the rest of these cold and greedy robots? Who are these executioners, and how do they live with themselves? I know that these people don't feel guilty for committing even the worst acts. They tell themselves they are just obeying orders, and this keeps them from asking themselves moral and guilt-inducing questions. I read recently that it's psychologically comforting for the majority of human beings to submit to rules and ideologies. This is what prevents them from thinking and from feeling isolated if, by chance, they were ever struck by the sudden desire to revolt.

The industrial system and the globalization of cruelty mangle people's consciences while crushing animal lives. Animals are merely objects, machines, no longer living beings. So, whatever their motivations may be, *all* defenders of animal protection have my respect. For they are the rebels, they are the people who say NO to things that seem set in stone, to a cruelty that is organized and accepted by the greater majority, to an ideology where man is all-powerful and draws from the Earth's resources, exploiting animal life as much as he still can. I respect and embrace those who do not deanimalize animals and who do not dehumanize their own conscience.

A Trailblazing Battle

It is immoral, abnormal, and inhumane to cage animals inside the notion of inferiority. I have fought for them to be respected since the sixties; alas, this trailblazing cost me dearly. I was ridiculed; people despised me for what I was doing. They were brutal because I was Brigitte Bardot, and they didn't want to listen to me on this topic. It was also not the right moment to have that particular debate. I understand that clearly now. It wasn't a time when people felt like thinking about animal rights. And I think to them I was doing the same thing I had done in my films: something avant-garde and, therefore, an act of provocation. It was unthinkable, for certain people, that a beautiful woman at the height of her stardom would be thinking about animals and prancing around on television shows with slaughterhouse pistols. I shocked people and swept away preconceived ideas. When I filmed *And God Created Woman*,[4] I created a scandal of infinite proportions and changed the image of the woman and her place in film. Vadim's production style and the film's aesthetic also greatly influenced later filmmakers. It was the same with animals. Hearing my voice supporting their cause sounded futile, idiotic, or superficial to people at the time. Nevertheless, today people are willing to ask themselves about the meaning of their existence alongside us.

Demanding respect for animals has often been an affair for "intellectuals." I don't like this word because it very often implies a pretentiousness, minimizing the importance of experience. Nevertheless, I can only bow before the women and men who have offered their time and writings to this cause: Leonardo da Vinci, Marguerite Yourcenar, Romain Gary, Victor Hugo, Émile Zola, and Victor Schoelcher, who accelerated the abolition of human slavery in France. I salute the work of ethologists,[5] as well as the recent commitment of certain authors to animal protection. In their books, these beings all dream of a community of living things; they don't dissociate the animal cause from the cause of men. In spite of this, animal well-being has never been taken seriously and studied adequately in depth. Today, I can see that things are beginning to shift, and I hope that the work of these individuals will arouse this sense of calling in others.

The intellectuals of animal protection touch minds, whereas I am the animal protector in people's hearts. I do not differentiate between species; I am "antispeciesist" in body and soul, but for forty-four years I have

4 *And God Created Woman*, directed by Roger Vadim, 1956.
5 Ethology is the study of the behavior of animal species.

been proclaiming this in a different way than the thinkers, without scholarly terms.[6] My battle is physical and basic. Between my incandescent blondeness of yesterday and my rage today, I have never reaped great respect from intellectuals. Well, I don't mind. I draw my reflections from my experience and what I have lived.

I am happy to have been able to live long enough to see, read about, and touch with my own hands the debate around antispeciesism, the development of vegetarianism, and the growth of veganism. Sometimes when I am discouraged, when I am too impatient to see animal bondage abolished, I tell myself that things are coming to fruition just the same. By denouncing, protesting, and repeating the same things, and by being photographed with so many animals, I was able to touch people, and all of this entered into the collective unconscious. When I see organizations criticizing the cruelties of slaughterhouses, activists infiltrating bullfighting rings, or crowds blocking the arrival of a circus in their city, I sometimes tell myself—and with no pretension whatsoever, only tenderness and pride—that all of these people are a little bit, somehow, my children.

Whether one is an author, an activist, or an organization spokesperson, every voice that is raised against animal persecution will contribute to the advancement of this essential cause. According animals respect and the right to live is a matter of course and the logical evolution of our humanity.

Tears

I never cry. At least, not in public. I refuse to. For me, it would be a sign of weakness. I don't like to complain, and I am horrified by the

---

6 Antispeciesism is a school of thought that rejects the hierarchy between animal species, including man.

immodesty of emotions. I don't like sharing my deep pains with other people. Not even with my husband. Sometimes, though, in the quietness of my bedroom or the privacy of my office, I have allowed myself to let it out, to truly let go.

I am extremely emotional about many things, but real tears are only shed for the pain and suffering of others, never over my own fate. I cry about what shouldn't exist, about cruelty for the sake of destruction, barbarism, and injustice. I cry for the weak, humans and animals alike.

For the latter, my pain is more intense; it feels like my life is being sucked out of me. And God knows I have cried for them. So much so that during an appointment with an ophthalmologist, I learned that I no longer had any tears. My quota had been exceeded. Tears may come to my eyes from time to time, but now it is impossible for me to get them out. I no longer have this ability; my eyes are worn out from so much crying. Before 1973 and the beginning of my involvement in this cause, I used to be able to burst into long bouts of weeping. But I never felt as despondent as I did in 1977, after my first turbulent press conference with journalists and local hunters in Canada. One of them ambushed me with the body of a recently killed baby seal who was lying covered in blood inside a plastic bag. I rushed into another room and succumbed to a fit of wrenching tears, unending sobs. Alone in a corner, I cried out at human monstrosity.

That day, I understood that the greatest sufferings have no sound, and that it is useless to put them on display.

It was in the same country, nearly thirty years later, that heavy and abundant tears fell once more down my face. Once again, I was at a press conference, pleading with everything I had that they put an end to the massacre of seals. And the intensity of my words was such that emotion overtook me. No one understood what was wrong with me; I was in pain, psychologically and physically, at the thought that these journalists were not understanding what I was saying. And the tears came out all by themselves, like a voiceless accusation. I cried in front of everyone. And not just heavy sobs, but tears. Tears of battle.

The Founding Battle: Baby Seals

In retrospect, I realize that the choice to take care of animals is more than a direction I chose for my life; it is a mission, that of helping the other and my fellow animal. It is something I am required to do.

The symbol of my battle remains the baby seals. I am known worldwide for the photograph taken of me in 1977 on the ice floe with a *blanchon*. The French term comes from the magnificent coat of white fur on these small animals that allows them to hide more easily on the ice. After having been "hatched" and nursed by his mother for several weeks, the *blanchon* will become a seal and his waterproof fur will turn gray. Baby seals are extremely vulnerable, particularly when their mothers leave to go fishing. During this time, they remain on the ice alone, wrapped warmly in their fur and in their fear of becoming prey for numerous predators such as bears and, of course, humans. Hunting *blanchon*s is disturbingly easy because they don't fight back: they've been in existence for barely two weeks. They are babies, and they innocently allow themselves to be approached by hunters before they are clubbed and then dismembered, often while they are still alive. The weapons used, called "hakapiks," consist of a metal tip for smashing the seal's skull and a long meat hook for dragging the small creature's body over the ice. He's a baby, fragile, waiting for his mother, and then he is skinned alive. The mothers, powerless, remain beside the little bald and bloody body for several days, trembling and trying to warm it against them and sometimes to nurse it, because this is the only way they know to give life to their baby.

This is why the battle for animals involves morality. This is why I had no choice but to get involved.

Beauty and Kindness

"How marvelous it is that beauty and grace are, at the same time, kindness."[7] It is with these words that the writer Marguerite Yourcenar ends a letter she sent me on February 24, 1968. In it, she was asking me to use my global reputation to condemn the seal massacres. My intervention on behalf of the slaughterhouse animals had convinced her that I would be the perfect advocate to persuade women to abandon their fur garments. In her letter—lively, profound, and dedicated, just like she was— she told me how the fur industry thrived upon the pain and agony of animals; she spoke about "brutality" and man's "savage cruelty" to achieve his own ends. She asked me to reach out to the Canadian prime minister and to do whatever I could to condemn the exploitation of sealskin.

I set about doing so nine years later, never thinking for a moment that someone out in the world had already thought of me as the person to lead this battle. This is because, as fate would have it, I did not receive that letter until much later. When I eventually met Marguerite Yourcenar one epic evening, she reminded me about the letter she had sent and was surprised by my incomprehension: "But wasn't I the one who encouraged you to go out on the ice?"

In 1980, Marguerite Yourcenar became the first woman elected to the Académie française. She had barely finished giving her inaugural speech when she was asked if there was anything she wished for. She responded: "To meet Brigitte Bardot." Living in solitude at La Madrague, I must confess that going to Paris annoyed me. I obviously respected this woman, but I hadn't read anything by her and I usually tried to avoid these kinds of invitations: the cocktail parties and cozy rendezvous. I declined her invitation, but this didn't throw her off. On the contrary,

---

7 Marguerite Yourcenar, *Lettres à ses amis et quelques autres*, Gallimard, 1995.

one stormy evening after coming back from La Garrigue, muddy and
wet from head to toe and surrounded by my dogs, who were no less of a
mess than I was, I was starting to light a fire when my security guard
informed me that a lady was at the door. At this hour and with all
this rain?

"Who is it?"

"She says her name is Marguerite Yourcenar."

I let her in; she was soaking wet, holding an umbrella and wearing
boots. She was accompanied by her chauffeur. I welcomed her, and we
kissed each other on the cheek as if we had always been dear friends.
Marguerite Yourcenar had come to see me without telling me to make
sure I couldn't say no. She had certainly figured me out! After we both
dried off, we uncorked a bottle of champagne and talked for three or four
hours. I offered her some vegetable soup on the waterproof tablecloth in
my kitchen, which she couldn't accept because she was expected at a dinner with Gaston Defferre, the mayor of Marseille. I enjoyed this intimate
connection with Marguerite Yourcenar. Our discussion was simple and
profound. I had La Madrague, and she had Petite-Plaisance, a house in
the United States that she thought of as her refuge. She worked there in
peace, surrounded by her four-legged companions. Later she sent me her
books, taking care not to pass along any that were too complicated.
Marguerite Yourcenar understood me. She told me ahead of time that I
was going to be bored stiff by *Memoirs of Hadrian*,[8] her major work
and the book that brought her worldwide success. We never saw each
other again, but I maintained a long correspondence with her until her
death.

---

8 *Mémoires d'Hadrien*, Plon, 1951.

"B.B. Phoque/B.B. Seal"

It was when I saw the terrifying images of massacred seals on television that I decided to go to Canada. In the early seventies, news articles stated that the killings involved between 150,000 and three hundred thousand seals each year. The seals were killed mainly for their skin and fur, used in the fashion industry, as well as for their fat and oil, useful in the pharmaceutical industry. Not to mention their penises, which were used to make a powder that is still used as an aphrodisiac in Asian countries.

In April 1976, without my foundation and with only my celebrity as a weapon, I helped launch an enormous international campaign and led a protest in front of the Embassy of Norway, another country involved in the massacres. I didn't suspect that hostility was already brewing against me on the cobbled streets of Paris, but it was nothing compared with what I would experience across the Atlantic.

In the deafening silence that was all around, I was going to have to wage an all-out war against these ice butchers. I found my chance in 1977 by offering to help Franz Weber, a Swiss journalist, ecologist, and defender of seals, among other creatures. My letter dated February 17 was like a bottle thrown into the ocean; I told him that my time, my name, my money, and my person were at his disposal, and I assured him of my desire to "conquer human stupidity." I didn't beat around the bush because I needed him to feel something and to understand how determined I was. I was successful.

We met and decided to pool our collective strengths for a globally televised demonstration that he wanted to organize in the very places where the hunts took place, in March of that year. So we set off together—accompanied by a television crew, organizer Hubert Henrotte, and Mirko, my companion—for the small town closest to the ice floe on the eastern coast of Canada. After a few days on-site—with Canadian boycotts, meetings with hunting representatives, a heated press conference, and several attempts to land a helicopter on the ice floe—I was able, in the final hours of my trip, to hold a baby seal against me. His innocence and purity stayed with me for the rest of my life.

That day, in that landscape of marvels and desolation that is the Arctic ice, in those few minutes body-to-body with the baby seal I would never see again, I promised myself that I would spend my existence trying to save theirs. When I returned to France, exhausted, beaten down, but also strengthened by my experience, I already felt that I was no longer really the same. Something had grown in me—a certain seriousness had appeared in my voice; my gaze was sharper. My battle had taken root. I was starting to sense what I had been created for, and growing in my awareness of being inhabited by and for the animal being.[9]

This battle taught me everything I know about my "calling" as an animal defender. What I did *not* expect is that the battle would be carried out not only in the field, but also in the beautifully gilded chambers of national and European government bodies. I had been deeply moved during my trip by a considerable show of support from French President Giscard d'Estaing, who had recently banned the importation of *blanchon* skins in France. The following year, I was invited to the Council of Europe to plead the case of baby seals and to fight for a European embargo. I was entering another dimension: before, I had been an actress—sparkling on the red carpets, doing light interviews where I always made sure to get out a few witty remarks, sharing my life with artists and dandies—and now, I was speaking, arguing, and trying to convince steely-eyed men wearing perfectly tailored suits. I was forced to take on this political battle the way I always took on situations in which I found myself uncomfortable: in a natural manner. Even when I

---

9 Brigitte Bardot describes her 1977 trip to Canada at length in *Le Carré de Pluton*, Grasset, 1999.

spoke at international summits, I remained the same. The only thing
that mattered to me was animal life. I had a few technical concepts, numbers, and testimonies to support what I was saying, but it was my sincerity that remained essential to my pleas to make this massacre stop. In
those days, just like today, it was not with statistics that people's hearts
were won, even if they happened to be sitting in offices.

This first chapter in the fight against animal cruelty successfully led
to Europe closing its borders to *blanchon* furs in 1983. This victory was
made even sweeter by the steep decrease in hunting that followed the
ban. In 1987, faced with the collapse of the seal industry, Canada finally
outlawed *blanchon* hunting.[10]

My defense of the seals would become a recurring theme in my battle,
for the years of respite those poor creatures enjoyed were short. In 1995,
Canada took up intensive hunting once more, not for *blanchons* this
time, but for "juveniles," "adolescent" animals twenty days old. I organized a press conference with my foundation in Paris and went to the
Norwegian and Canadian Embassies. Unfortunately, in the beginning
of the 2000s, the number of killings exploded.

In 2006, I decided to go back to Canada. Uprisings were springing up
all over the world, but the new Canadian prime minister, Stephen
Harper, refused to listen. My letters of petition to him were left unanswered. My petitions and requests to meet with UN Secretary-General
Kofi Annan also ended in failure. On February 14, lists of signatures
were delivered to the Canadian Embassy in Paris by Robert Hossein,
Candice Patou, Dany Saval, and Henry-Jean Servat—representatives of
the foundation, supporters, and longtime friends. Three days later, we
learned—stunned, shattered, and sickened—that the quota had been
increased.

---

10 Source: Fondation Brigitte Bardot, office of animal protection.

I was suffering from arthritis, but despite my fragile and aching legs, I decided to take my crutches to Ottawa, twenty-nine years after my first expedition onto the ice, to meet with the prime minister. On Tuesday, March 21, a plane taking off from Roissy heading to Ottawa via London brought us closer to the Canadian chill. To call it that is an understatement, but I was determined to go all the way to the end.

When we arrived, the immigration officers asked me to follow them for questioning, at which point I was interrogated about my intentions for two hours. I was made to wait standing and was met with sarcastic remarks when I requested meetings that, according to the officers, I would never have. They were unfortunately correct. Held in check by the cutthroat powers of the Canadian hunting lobbies, the prime minister did not want to receive me. Forced to pay two hundred Canadian dollars for a three-day visitor's visa, I complied and reiterated my request to meet Stephen Harper.

My first visit in 1977 had left a lingering bitter taste in a country that had since become divided between seal defenders and the upholders of an inalienable tradition. Even worse: rumor had it that I might attempt an assassination. What a ridiculous idea! I was I was nearly seventy-five years old and on crutches: I could have been knocked over by a feather. I nevertheless went to the prime minister's office and was welcomed coldly by the concierge, to whom I gave a letter. The response: "Outside." There I was shown a fax in which the head of government refused to see me under any circumstances. Speaking via telephone was also impossible. A conference organized for the next day was already causing a commotion.

Only Paul Watson—creator of Sea Shepherd and a faithful supporter of my Canadian campaigns after we met on the ice in 1977—was by my side for this trying meeting with the journalists. Paul had learned of my arrival in Canada and had come to lend a hand. I hadn't expected this at all: he would prove to be a vital source of support.

I had naively believed that people would be touched to see the old lady I was now. I was wrong. During the press conference with 250 journalists and seventeen television channels, all obviously rough on me, all obviously unflinching in their opinions, Paul stood quietly beside me. When fatigue overwhelmed me, or I couldn't find the words in English, he stepped in every single time and took up the baton with passion. I knew I was being listened to, and that my words needed to be clear, strong, and convincing. The act of denouncing an ancestral culture, even in the third millennium, drew hostility from the Canadians. We displayed unbearable images of the killings. I couldn't look at them. The martyred seals' cries of pain in the film made me tremble. The lights came back on, and everyone in the room was dumbfounded by my sorrow.

Unable to hold on any longer, delirious with desperation, I pleaded for this massacre to "cease before my death, so that at least my life will have been good for something." The media impact of this press conference was tremendous because it had been rebroadcasted live on Canadian and American channels.

Back in France, still emotional and tested by this trip, I was granted permission to attend a meeting of the European Commission with Stavros Dimas to raise awareness about the seal situation and the need to propose an embargo on all products derived from this massacre. At the same time, my foundation was demanding support from the European Parliament on a request to the Commission concerning a ban on all commerce linked to seals.

My meeting with Stavros Dimas was decisive. Physically, I no longer resembled the forty-two-year-old who had once stood before European authorities: this time, my steps were heavy, my silhouette imposing, and my breath short. But my determination remained intact. Drawing from my own emotion, wearing no makeup, but speaking from my heart, I explained to this man, who was listening closely, in an English that was not really English, what happened during the hunts and what the seal-skin business entailed. We also showed him videos of the massacres in Canada.

Whenever I revisit these memories, I feel shivers all over my body. The experience was so powerful because it really was a battle between life and death.

So, ignoring convention, as if I were speaking about my own life, about the survival of my own children, I begged and begged Stavros Dimas to do everything he could to make sure that the European Union (EU) would reject the importation of seal and pinniped skins and all products derived from them. Later, taking advantage of being at the European Commission, I visited the office of Markos Kyprianou, who was then working with my foundation on the closing of European borders to dog and cat fur. What we were on the verge of accomplishing for our pets—and we did accomplish it a few months later—we absolutely had to accomplish for the seals, as well.

In 2008, the European Commissioner chose Saint Brigitte's Day, July 23, to present his proposal for a regulation aiming to close European borders to products derived from the hunting of pinnipeds, in other words, seals, walruses, and sea lions. In his presentation to the press, Stavros Dimas paid tribute to my actions and those of my foundation. To support his proposal, he shared a damning statement from the European Food Safety Authority (EFSA), which explained that seals were some-times dismembered while still conscious, which led to a slow and painful death.

We had not imagined that such a step forward, as obvious as it seemed, would take so much patience and pugnacity, but each step of the process is critical for getting a law passed. After the commissioner's proposal, my foundation began the long task of lobbying European representatives. It was very effective. On May 5, 2009, I achieved the greatest victory of my battle: European regulations outlawing the importation and trade of seal products were adopted.

This decision was the final stamp on a thirty-year battle.

This immense victory—so symbolic, so powerful, and to me so crucial—gave me the unique satisfaction of being able to spare a few lives: no fewer than 350,000 seals each year, and several million since the adoption of the regulations.

The protection provided by the European embargo still stands, in spite of sharp criticism from Canada and Norway. The two countries continue to contest the European Union's ban, which became effective in 2010. The debate is always between defenders of the animal cause and hunters or others who profit from the life of pinnipeds and believe that, thanks to them, the animal population on the ice is regulated. Another of their arguments concerns the age-old traditions of the Inuit. We have always been careful to make a distinction between commercial hunting and traditional hunting, which does not actually involve baby seals, and only a handful of adult seals each year. It's not on the same scale, nor is it the same kind of cruelty! And finally, according to the fishermen, seals have the potential to become a threat to the environment because they are responsible for the decline in the cod population. As if pinnipeds were their only predators! Today, my foundation supports a wildlife care and rehabilitation center near Vancouver. Seals live there happily, and the majority are released back into the region they come from.

Even today, I am still overwhelmed by this progress, and at the same time, I can't let go of the bitter taste of having waited thirty years to get it. And sometimes I'm afraid: of time passing too quickly, of administrative sluggishness, of people's inertia, of the indifference of politicians. And yes, sometimes I am afraid that at eighty-three years of age I will never experience another victory for animals of this magnitude.

Chouchou

I still feel an infinite tenderness toward seals, and I cannot close this chapter without mentioning Chouchou. He was my little seal, but I couldn't keep him at my house in Bazoches; when he slept, he took up too much space in the henhouse, by the fireplace, or in the dog bed. He had become as big as my swimming pool. Unfortunately, at the time, no rescue centers existed like they do today, and I had to give Chouchou to Marineland in Antibes, which back then was not the frightening animal show park it is now. It was originally intended, on a small scale, to aid in the survival of the species.

Chouchou was such a character. He was given to me in 1976 by a French trawler from Newfoundland who had found him alone, abandoned, drifting on a piece of ice. I was asked to come to Fécamp to adopt him. I didn't hesitate for an instant.

Our first meeting inaugurated a long friendship. Little by little, his childish coat became gray, and Chouchou grew a lot. In Bazoches, he lived like a dog. I would throw the ball for the others, and my seal would run to get it with his flippers. The dogs would come and sleep around me, and Chouchou, too, demanded his share of snuggles, with his head resting on my shoulder.

My seal was so used to being mothered that it was always impossible to make him eat fish. He was used to drinking out of a bottle filled with cod liver oil and fish crushed in a blender. One day when I wanted to open his mouth to give him round fish—seals have to eat round fish, not flat, so the fish doesn't get stuck in their throats—he spit them right back onto my face. That smell of fish pulp stuck to my hair still turns my stomach today. Chouchou behaved like an eternal invalid, but he was growing so quickly; the adolescent of over 260 pounds that he had become could no longer be fed by bottle only. A friend of Paul-Émile Victor suggested that I separate myself from this massive adult and offer him a place with other seals who could show him how to eat fish. And this is how I made the decision to leave my Chouchou.

After giving him to the director of Marineland, I returned twice. I missed Chouchou terribly. The first time, when I arrived in front of the enclosure where he was tanning with his fellow seals, I made sure right away that the pool was spacious and that little shelters had been set up. One of them had even been christened "La Madrague." Chouchou immediately came toward me. This crushed me. I called his name: "Chouchou, come here my Chouchou!" I cried, he was coming, barreling in my direction with his fat flippers, letting out the cries of joy that are so typical of seals. I touched him, I kissed him, and then I left him, with the horrible feeling that I was abandoning him a second time. But I had no other choice. By the second and last of my visits, he had aged significantly and no longer recognized me. My calls, "Chouchou, my Chouchou," remained unanswered. I looked at him, slumped on the ground. He was a seal, he was old, and I was not there to accompany him during his final years. And then one day, the park informed me of his passing. Chouchou had died peacefully at twenty years old. When I hung up the telephone, I sat down. I lowered my head and tears streamed down my cheeks, all the way to my hands, which I was squeezing together to keep in the hollow of my palms the warm and comforting memory of my beloved seal's coat.

Woman on the Battlefield

My first trip to Canada gave me the taste and the need for being on the battlefield. When I decided to enlist in the battle for animals, I was hoping to go and tackle situations head-on, to see with my own eyes the unspeakable and the unavoidable. Until very recently, I needed to expose things, to see them, and if I didn't go where things were happening, I knew that I might be lacking conviction in my emotions and legitimacy in the eyes of others. I needed to have seen in order to say, "This is disgusting, this is appalling, this is sad," with adequate desperation. Most of the time I was fighting: at times against walls, at other times against real or imaginary enemies. This battle is hard and long, and after a while I learned how to find a chink in the armor and convey my emotion.

I don't know where this will lead, but I never let anything go; I go to the end of everything I undertake. One of my longest battles has been focused on hippophagy. I have been fighting for nearly fifty years, but nothing is budging, in spite of my proposals for legislation and my condemnations. In spite of this lack of inertia, I will go all the way to the end. And perhaps even beyond.

Apart from the seals, one of my most horrible memories is from 1981. It was Christmas Eve, and I had come to a shelter in Longpré-les-Amiens in the Somme region. A letter had been sent to me to report the unsanitary conditions at the location and the nightmarish life of the animals incarcerated there. I was accompanied, among others, by Liliane Sujansky, the great protector of animals who directed the Société protectrice des animaux (SPA), and Allain Bougrain-Dubourg. We didn't know what we were about to discover, but what we saw that night went far beyond what we could have imagined. Roughly sixty dogs were eating one another, and a female was giving birth while the others devoured the puppies coming out of her belly. Twenty cats were dying of coryza, a serious infection. Like true outlaws, armed with crowbars, we pried open the dog cages to save the ones we still could. This rescue was being performed without authorization and was done as a matter of extreme urgency in the middle of the night. Just when we were about to leave, I saw a dog wasting away at the back of her crate, and knew I had to save her. I couldn't manage to open her cage, and the others yelled that I had to leave her behind. I didn't want to; I couldn't run away and abandon this dog and her silent pleas. I grabbed a large rock to bust open the rusty lock, and it gave way under my determination. The dog jumped on me, and we left running. But then I realized that we hadn't been able to rescue the cats who were shivering in a freezing cattery that was equipped with a single wheezing electric radiator. We were going as fast as our legs could carry us, but we could still hear those poor victims coughing, sneezing, and dying. There was nothing we could do; we couldn't save them all. So we left them. And this wound is still open more than thirty-five years later. Not helping suffering animals at a moment when I could have made me feel like howling at the moon. We put dozens of dogs into trucks with heated crates that the SPA had arranged for us. I myself packed no fewer than ten dogs into my Range Rover. On that cold and mysterious Christmas Eve, lost in the plains of Picardy, we had left hell behind to give these dogs, who were yapping with joy, a more dignified life. At the same time, other little cats were meowing their last breaths . . . I had never felt angrier.

I began to feel in myself a rage that grew each year in my heart and in my gut. A rage that moved mountains but that could also be indifferent toward other people. It is an anger that mounts inside me like a power from somewhere else; it's capable of the best things, and sometimes the worst.

My beginnings in animal activism were spent in the company of the wonderful Liliane Sujansky. It was with her that I went to the Zoo de Vendeuil near Amiens: an open-air death house. This was November 1988. Monkeys, wolves, panthers, and lions—or, more accurately, their shivering carcasses—were dying in the cold. We rescued over a hundred animals and placed them in parks like the one directed by Christian Huchedé at Refuge de l'Arche in the Mayenne region.

Roger Macchia, president of the Center for the Shelter and Protection of Mistreated Equine Species (CHEM), was with me when my eyes were opened to the cruel treatment of horses sent to the slaughterhouse. I saw terrifying convoys between Poland and France of animals who were no more than shadows of themselves. I will return later to this tragedy, which is among my most gut-wrenching battles.

Each new discovery made me more desperate than ever. When we decide to take part in this kind of battle, we must make sure our heart is well attached, because each new revelation shatters the heart and spirit. All of the sites that are visited and the meetings that are organized possess their own sense of gravity and give rise to their own questions, but I still don't have any of the answers. How can we let this happen?

In the beginning of 1991, eighty wolves from Hungary had been selected for use in the fur industry or to be stuffed and put on display at a museum in Budapest. The mayor of the city called my tiny little foundation for help. Once again, Liliane was extraordinary: armed with a team created just for this task, trucks, ministerial authorizations, and veterinary approvals, she organized and accompanied a convoy for three days and nights to save the wolves. On March 2, 1991, I met them in Lozère, where Gérard Ménatory would be welcoming the animals to his Parc du Gévaudan. The morning of my departure, Europe 1 gave me the news that Serge Gainsbourg had died. I will remember for the rest of my life that shattered feeling: this battle for life, the saving of a wild animal, and the disappearance of a dear being, a man I had loved, also wild, and so sensitive, unfit for the elementary day-to-day of mere mortals and, in the end, for life here on Earth. When I got to the park, Gérard invited me into an enclosure with five wild she-wolves. Alone and in pain, I remained seated among them. The females sniffed me, almost caressing me. Their kindness was extraordinary, as was their ability to sense how I was feeling. A few tears streamed from the corners of my eyes. They contained a tremendous world of suppressed pain. The wolves could feel it. They stayed with me. In that suspended moment, I was no longer myself; I was in communion with animals because they could sense me. I was on all fours, as one must be before a wolf, and one of the females licked my mouth while another tried to catch a flower stuck in my chignon. I turned around slowly, very slowly, so I wouldn't frighten her, and met her intense, yellow-green gaze.

Unlike dogs, whom we domesticate, the wolf dominates us; his fleeting glance and aerial movements make him the wild beast par excellence. I willingly accept his power and his desire for conquest. And if I had to live on all fours before a wolf forever, I would do it. This episode in my life is one of the great encounters that confirmed my choice and reinforced my belief that animality is an extraordinary world we know nothing about apart from what we choose to learn and what is useful for us. After the moment with wolves I've just described, how can we doubt for a moment their conscience and compassion?

La Fondation Brigitte Bardot (FBB)

I often compare my battle to a calling. I don't think this is too far off the mark. It is very troublesome, sometimes more hopeless than glorifying, and a capacity for self-sacrifice is critical. Animal protection is a religion. Everything stemmed from a conviction I had: humanity is not at the center of the world, animals are not men's slaves, and subjugating and mistreating them makes us inhumane.

Deciding to take up this cause and leaving cinema was the easiest part; then I had to create the framework for my rebellion. I learned year by year, day by day, and I am still learning. At first, I attended trainings with organizations like the SPA and the French Animal Rights League (LFDA). The bulk of my activities were focused on my visits to shelters where I supported the residents, adopting some and bringing them home with me to Bazoches. This is how I met my sheep, Nénette, and my donkey, Cornichon, whom I saved from the slaughterhouse. I was popular enough at the time to still be in demand in the media, and I was invited onto feature programs like *Aujourd'hui Madame* in 1974, *Au pied du mur* in 1975, *Les Dossiers de l'écran* in 1980, and *Entre chien et loup* with Allain Bougrain-Dubourg in 1987. I believed in exposure, in "hype," in the power of repeated words, and in constant condemnation.

My idea was to create an organization to gain the credibility and recognition I was hoping for concerning the animal condition. Being completely new to everything administrative, including paperwork, accounts, laws, etc., throughout the seventies, I kept myself surrounded by the same team: my mother, my friends, and Michèle, my secretary, who all helped bring this project to fruition. I was throwing them into a set of circumstances that was very different from what ours had been up to that point. But did they love me? Well, then they would embrace my battle! In 1976, with the help of Philippe Cottereau, Paul-Émile Victor loaned me a room in his set of offices in Saint-Cloud, a western suburb of Paris. But dubious financial arrangements and profits that were too scarce, or else falling directly into the hands of the creditors of Paul-Émile Victor's organization, rapidly transformed this beautiful venture into a failure that cost me dearly. The still-meager funds of my brand-new organization were being used to pay for Paul-Émile Victor's office expenses! Until that moment, I had an immense trust in this man and an unlimited respect for him; from then on, I broke off all contact with him and was very disappointed. As for my organization, I had to pay everything back out of my own pocket, including reimbursements to donors and other individuals who had sent me money. Once these things were sorted out, I sent everyone packing. If it was going to be like this, I was not going to be dependent on anyone else and would do everything alone!

Along with these bureaucratic concerns, I continued my visits in the field until 1977, when coverage of my first Canadian battle was broadcast across the world. I suddenly became the *pasionaria* of seals and the animal protection cause. With this exposure, I met the bigwigs in this arena: Allain Bougrain-Dubourg and Liliane Sujansky I have already mentioned, but there was also Bruno Laure[11] and professor Jean-Claude Nouët,[12] to whom I offered my celebrity in order to bring one item or another into the public eye. With their authority and my aura combined, we were able to open the doors of ministries, but that's as far as we got! I would discover little by little the lead wall of politics. The doors would open for Brigitte Bardot, but unfortunately, I was often looked at but rarely listened to. I understood that animal protection did not interest very many people, and that the keyword for this kind of activism was "perseverance."

I revisit this period in the second volume of my memoirs, *Pluto's Square*. I do not regret this title, because it accurately describes a very difficult astral rendezvous in which, between the ages of forty and fifty, I had to combat the forces of possession. I made it through, but it still brings back bitter memories. My foundation is ultimately a success story; I had managed it practically on my own. This was a period when I was very isolated, without a husband, without parents (Maman had passed in 1978), and no railing to cling to. So many times, I felt like letting all of it go. All of the administrative work required was beyond me. Those ten years between the midseventies and the mideighties, this Pluto's Square, were the most difficult of my life, a real crossing of the desert. And to top it all off, breast cancer decided to announce itself. I remember those hours of gnawing pain, those medical appointments, the operation to scrape my lymph nodes, and this terrible paradox: I was still Brigitte Bardot to the world, yet I felt abandoned. Who could have imagined at

---

11 President of LAF-DAM, the French antivivisection league—Defenders of abused animals, which then merged with Aequalis to become Talis, then One Voice.
12 Founder, honorary chairman, and president of the Animal Rights Foundation.

that time that Juliette from *And God Created Woman* or the Harley-Davidson sex symbol was living more like a recluse than ever at La Madrague? I could no longer move my left arm. I was in pain, so much pain. And then my caretaker decided it would be a good idea to leave me. For the first time in my life, but at the very worst possible moment, I was taking care of my own home, emptying my own trash with a screwed-up breast and a useless arm.

This decade was like the "negative" of my life; after an out-of-the-ordinary existence of light, success, and glory, it was as if everything were being taken back from me . . . and there were probably a few things I needed to understand. After a period of splendor, I would have to endure certain trials like everyone else. I should have died, but I made it through. I believe that I didn't necessarily deserve what happened to me, but the obstacles I had to climb over were the highest I had ever encountered. My life is like that: everything or nothing, extreme glory or extreme despair, extreme love or extreme loathing that people feel for me. Between the two there are choices, stages to go through, and encounters with others, too. Between the two there is a balance to be found, and it is this search that is, most likely, the prerequisite for wisdom.

In 1986, I tried once again to found my own organization. This one would be formed "at home" and with what was on hand: I used a small guest bedroom at La Madrague as my office, and a lawyer from Saint-Tropez, along with my secretary and friend, Gloria, accompanied me on this new journey. Then Charles Pasqua, minister of the interior at the time, explained to me that an organization was all well and good, but the firepower of a foundation was without comparison. In order to obtain such a title, though, an organization would have to have access to a capital of three million francs that were not to be touched, the famous "funds" of the "foundation."

I couldn't scrape together an amount like that; the majority of my earnings as a star had been squandered earlier, and there was no longer any money coming in. Then, somehow, between April and June 1987, I managed to set myself up in the market in Saint-Tropez from 6:30 to 11:00 a.m. selling a pile of trinkets I'd inherited from my life as a star. On June 17, 1987, everything of value I possessed was put on auction at the Maison de la Chimie in Paris. My guitar, the jewels Günter[13] had given me, my dress from my wedding to Vadim, silverware, and furniture. My objects, a part of my soul, passed before my eyes and left me. My first life made room for my second.

That day, without any preparation, as I was handed the microphone, I spoke the words that went down in history: "I gave my beauty and my youth to men. I am going to give my wisdom and experience to animals." I had regained control of my life and of myself. I was leaving the stations of the cross, the hesitant steps that had peppered the beginning of my battle, and I was becoming a warrior, the open hand and the closed fist, ready to fight animal injustice.

My friend Liliane Sujansky left the SPA and joined me to run my brand-new foundation. In 1988, we settled in Paris at 4 rue Franklin.

Once again, my animal "career" really took off thanks to television. Two journalist friends of mine from long ago, Jean-Louis Remilleux and Roland Coutas, suggested that I host a series of programs about animals. Fifteen years after fleeing the cameras, I would have to offer myself to them again, but this time for the right cause. For three years, from 1989 to 1992, on *S.O.S. Animaux*, television segments about elephants, animals being hunted and butchered, laboratory guinea pigs, sea mammals, animals used for fur, horses, dogs, cats, and the great apes condemned human cruelty, and no one was spared, not even the weak-stomached. Years before the unbearable images that can be seen on the Internet

---

13 Fritz Gunter Sachs, BB's third husband, was a German photographer, author, industrialist.

today, our program on TF1 showed the unspeakable. The audience grew quickly, as did Minitel memberships. My foundation was finally well known.

In the end, the date that is most symbolic of my self-sacrifice for the cause is still February 21, 1992. A decree in the *Journal Officiel* stipulated that La Madrague, my mythical property in Saint-Tropez raved about all over the world, had been given to the foundation. This was how we obtained the capital necessary for its recognition of public utility. We were then able to take legal action and file lawsuits and could also accept donations and legacies, which are so essential to the functioning of a foundation.

Women and Men

I am very proud of the Fondation Brigitte Bardot and the people who work there. When I enter the headquarters in Paris today, at 28 rue Vineuse, I am blown away. I never seem to realize that I am at the base of this body of one hundred employees in Paris, with thousands of donors, delegates, and volunteer researchers all over France.

I think that the geographic placement of the foundation has brought me luck because it is at the heart of my family history. Not only are the offices located two steps away from one of the apartments I loved most on Avenue Paul-Doumer, but even more miraculously, they are just across from 39 rue Vineuse, where the Parisian seat of Usines Air Liquide was located, which was managed by my father and his brothers. What is today a modern building was once a small private hotel that housed within its walls the offices of Bardot and Cie. The only vestige of this past is a small garden where I used to love playing with my sister. This space still exists. It is still the same: horrible! I have kept and framed the paper with the letterhead that reads: "Société Bardot et Cie, 39 rue

Vineuse, Paris 16e." I can't help but see a sign in this proximity to my foundation as a sort of paternal and protective presence.

For the almost thirty-two years that my foundation has existed, I have always hoped to preserve a family ambiance, a generosity like my own in its ranks. The FBB must preserve and defend its human dimension, even if the "familial" side undeniably brings with it its own advantages and inconveniences. You know, family stuff.

So, even in Saint-Tropez, I work with them every day. We are constantly in contact. I go to Paris about every two years, and I don't miss it. Everything today is electronic: I work on the journals from a distance, I check the photos, the text, the captions, the formatting. I am aware, however, of the enthusiasm that is triggered by each of my appearances on rue Vineuse. This is why I go. People are constantly stopping by, and it's a real motivation for them to meet me. It's a source of human warmth, a presence that can help them feel justified in their commitment to the cause. People are often intimidated when they meet me, so I put them at ease. I offer them a little drink and off we go!

Today, the position of director is held by Ghyslaine Calmels-Bock, an excellent manager, who is a determined and very demanding woman. Ghyslaine has all the qualities of a director and manages the day-to-day work with intelligence, leading the foundation with a masterful hand. She has created shelters equipped with catteries, infirmaries, and quarantine areas that bear no resemblance to prisons. She also takes care of the legacies, inheritances, and donations we are given. Ghyslaine has the upright character needed for this kind of battle.

Franck, my secretary, is both my friend and my partner. I have known him for over twenty years, and he is very attentive to so many things. Franck is one of the few people who visits me regularly. He comes every month to bring me mail, bills, letters to be sent, and other work.

And last, Christophe Marie is responsible for animal protection and is the foundation's spokesperson. He has the same birthday as I, September 28. There is a great affection between us. He is like my son. I think of everyone who works at the foundation as my children, not as employees. I have a blind trust in them, but I still look over everything of great importance. Of course, the day-to-day work is done without me. But when a large case requires a public statement or a certain kind of action, we decide with Christophe what should be done. The majority of the time, I draft letters with him to certain chiefs of government and foreign presidents. I don't let anything major happen without stamping my "pawprint" on it—my way of writing, which, I admit, is rather unique. It's true that I don't write like everyone else. I don't want the letters coming from my foundation to carry a cold and administrative tone. We're talking about humanity, about lives, about beings suffering; it is critical to me that the words exude that. I write the way I speak, the way I think. One letter I sent to Nicolas Hulot concluded with "A little annoyed, I send my love." This is *my* kind of closing salutation. Naturally, that was not what Christophe would have written.

Christophe is a pillar of this foundation. He is indispensable to me. The foundation would not be what it is without him. He is of the highest importance and is my natural successor. He's a fighter, like me, but he possesses a few superior assets: he is diplomatic and tactical, which I am not at all. I unload everything I have to say, never burdening myself with what people might think, whereas he is able to regulate my impulses. We complement each other extremely well.

This kind of antiwaffling that I practice serves the interests of my foundation. This may not always be the case, but it is part of my character, my personality; people like me that way. If I were to become diplomatic, I would no longer be interesting. Even though it can frighten people, this all-the-way-to-the-end mentality has nevertheless been use-ful. At the end of 2012, we learned that the administrative tribunal in Lyon had just sentenced two elephants to death because they were sus-pected of having tuberculosis. After taking part in the glory days of Cirque Pinder, Baby and Népal would have to die amidst deafening indifference. I accused anyone and everyone in a long letter: the circus, a hotbed of animal slavery; zoos, which parade wild animals around in miserable conditions and do not intervene to curb their extinction; and finally, the French state, which was once again "dropping its pants" for the people who wanted to go about their business against the advice of animal protection organizations. We then solicited the arbitration of Minister of Agriculture Stéphane Le Foll, offering to take in the ele-phants ourselves. At the beginning of 2013, I asked President Hollande to pardon the animals condemned to death. Demonstrations, letters, and newspaper editorials did nothing. So, I made a statement that if Baby and Népal were euthanized, I would follow Gérard Depardieu and also leave France to become a Russian national. I said I was ashamed of my country, that it had become nothing but a cemetery for animals. This letter was picked up by all of the French and foreign media outlets. And I can tell you that at that moment, nothing was going to stop me: I was set on going to dance the *kazochok* with my crutches! Finally, in the spring, the administrative tribunal in Lyon cancelled the prefecture's order that had authorized the slaughter of the two elephants. They were transferred into the care of Princess Stéphanie of Monaco, at her request, and were brought to a park created for them in the hills above the princi-pality, where they underwent new serological tests. This is how Baby and Népal were saved.

Yes, I take things all the way to the end; I get angry, I condemn, I exag-gerate, because I don't feel like compromising who I am. I wouldn't be able to because it's what personifies me, and also because I would be afraid of opting for the bureaucratic tone that always used to scare me off. Nature in its literal sense, the nature of animals, like my own, can be improved. But never changed.

What Does My Foundation Do?

My foundation leads a great number of battles every day, and they are battles without borders and without distinctions between species. Often, and rightly so, most of the public sees us as an adoption agency for dogs and cats, even though we have extended our activities to many other causes. Thanks to our work, beginning with Christophe, we try day after day to make a difference, to take our voice to political spaces and decision-makers. Wild animals being one of our priorities, we have financed the construction of a wild animal hospital in Chile, as well as a park to care for mistreated bears in Bulgaria, for koalas in Australia, for elephants in Thailand, and for horses in Tunisia. If the foundation wasn't active, a great many species conservation programs would be non-existent, such as those concerned with chimpanzees, bonobos, and gorillas in Africa, or gibbons in Asia. We also work hand in hand with other organizations, like Sea Shepherd. Paul Watson and I share the same outlook on the world, the same indignation. From our time on the ice in 1977 to today, it has been obvious that we should combine our strengths. In 2010, my foundation financed a several-weeks-long mission to the Faroe Islands to fight against the killing of cetaceans. The cooperation with Sea Shepherd was renewed again in 2014 with a new mission to the same area, where hundreds of pilot whales are hemmed into bays to be massacred in a blood-red sea. And, since 2011, the trimaran christened *Brigitte Bardot* has taken part in Paul Watson's nongovernmental organization (NGO) campaigns against Japanese whalers.

Throughout the world, we try to give financial support to projects that are near to our hearts. In 2002, we launched our first mobile veterinary clinic to sterilize, vaccinate, and tattoo hundreds of stray dogs in Serbia. In Bhutan, in 2008, we took part in the construction of a kennel that could welcome animals in better conditions the purchase of a vehicle to collect food, and the construction of a veterinary clinic. That same year, the FBB also cofinanced the Valitox program in collaboration with the Pro Anima Scientific Committee. This program allows tests to be performed in order to find an alternative to using animals in experimentation with toxic products. I'll come back to this.

In this area, as in many others, animal organizations must become influential groups; this has been my conviction from the beginning. For this reason, the FBB is very involved with major national and international bodies like the Ministry of Agriculture, the European Parliament, and the Convention on International Trade in Endangered Species of Wild Fauna and Flora.

In France, the foundation helps many shelters in need, conducts large-scale sterilization campaigns for stray cats, and saves as many horses as possible from the slaughterhouses, along with ponies, cows, and sheep also destined to cruel fates. We do not only rescue animals; we also house them. This is because it was always inconceivable for me to simply release a rescued animal immediately—risking throwing him into a vicious cycle—and because we have the means. My wealth is entirely at the disposal of my foundation and the animals it cares for.

My Homes Are Their Homes

My houses have always been a refuge for me. It is obvious, then, that they would become the same for my animals. I've always hated traveling, even when I was an actress. Especially because during that period, I was leaving "home" for faraway lands to do a job I didn't enjoy. I remember in particular my departure for the Almeria Desert in Spain to film a western called *Shalako*.[14] I had been enjoying a beautiful love affair with Serge Gainsbourg and now was being dragged away to a soulless and hostile place. My soul was whole and at peace in the privacy of my house, which was my burrow. I am a wild animal, and deep down I always have this desire for protection, for folding inward into the universe I know.

The only FBB refuge in which I have never lived myself is La Mare Auzou in the Eure region. All I did was choose it. I visited this marvelous place on a day of glacial cold. The fog was keeping me from making out the details of the site, until a royal stag approached my car. I contemplated the animal's majesty for a few long minutes, and our eyes met. Without fear, he stared at me the same way I had stared at him. This unique and wild moment was a revelation for me. La Mare Auzou would be a new land of refuge for homeless animals. This was 1992. Today, it is a haven of peace for almost one thousand domestic and farm animals like dogs, cats, horses, pigs, donkeys, sheep, and cows. We have a sheepfold, a solarium, an infirmary, places to rest . . . in short, a veritable realm to foster the resilience of the animal being.[15]

The last but not the least of the refuges, which has belonged to my foundation since 2006, is located in Bazoches-sur-Guyonne in the Yvelines region. I bought this property in 1960, just after the birth of my son, Nicolas. This period was characterized by an intense need for calm and a rejection of any kind of hysteria directed at me. This new house represented my desire to live normally, naturally, to share a cocoon with my son. Even if life had other plans.

---

14 *Shalako*, directed by Edward Dmytryk, 1968.
15 Resilience is a psychiatric concept popularized by Boris Cyrulnik and defined as the capacity to reconstruct oneself after a significant trauma.

In Bazoches, I always felt like Snow White in the heart of her glade. The thatched roof that covered the house practically down to the ground had a lot to do with it: it looked like a huge mushroom. It was an old sheepfold from the eighteenth century built from cob, and the walls were a mixture of mud and plaster.

Bazoches was my farm, a place of peace and well-being par excellence. When I was filming, the producers only allowed us Sundays off, so as soon as Saturday came, I would beat it for Bazoches! That house was a real wreck! But my God, how I loved it. Cut off from everything, I relaxed on long walks with my dogs and lit bonfires. Bazoches matched the most secret dream of my younger years: to possess an isolated place in the country and live there by myself, without any fuss, surrounded by animals I had taken in to give them a second chance at life. And that is what I did. I picked up all of the creatures who were hanging around, the ones no one wanted. I saved a sheep headed for the slaughterhouse whom a little girl had asked me to adopt. Since I didn't yet have anywhere for him to stay, I put him in my kitchen temporarily. Well before starting my foundation, on my way out of a studio one day, I went to the SPA in my Rolls-Royce, a magnificent car equipped with a pane of glass separating the driver from the passengers. I returned to Bazoches with seven dogs and eight cats. I was in the back, buried under the balls of fur, and cats were climbing on my chauffeur's head or winding between his legs. The poor man made sure at all costs not to swerve too much. When we arrived at our destination, all of the animals hurled themselves toward the door to taste their new freedom. The act of releasing these dogs and cats—dirty, shabby, and haggard—who were still encaged in minuscule enclosures a few hours before was, for me, a moment of extraordinary happiness.

To flee the Tropézien buzz, I spent all of my summers in Bazoches. Then, over the years, I would lengthen my stays. I have not set foot in that house in the country since 2006 when I donated it to my foundation. This was my choice. Now, the marvelous house that gave me so much pleasure no longer belongs to me. Of course, I think about the place, and I sometimes miss it, because it resembled me from top to bottom. I have never felt as much myself and at home anywhere else. But I refuse to fall into nostalgia; I don't want to miss a place, especially when it has become so indispensable to animal rescue. Bazoches is far more significant and useful with me no longer there. My Seven Dwarfs house is today the reason animals are alive, after it had been mine. What could be more natural, therefore, than sweeping away any kind of melancholy?

Finally, there is one house that has always stuck with me, for it is a part of me, just as I am a part of its walls: La Madrague. I believe this house always remained the fisherman's hut that I acquired in 1958, even though I've done a number of things to it and the end result is less rustic. But the house is just as welcoming as it was then. And if I need the countryside, I have La Garrigue, my farm just above it that unmistakably resembles the ambiance that reigned at Bazoches. La Madrague is very small. People who visit me are always surprised by the place's modesty; they always imagine that they are entering a star's universe, a sparkling villa on the water's edge. This is not the case.

I chose to settle definitively at La Madrague and to most likely finish my days there because it is the oldest of my houses. It is here that I have the most memories, the most lives and moments spent. I believe strongly in what a person leaves behind in a house, in the waves that pass through it, in the places where we feel comfortable or, on the contrary, ill at ease. La Madrague will forever represent my path, my highs and my lows. Everything is there: my youth, my extravagance, my overindulgences, my loves, my success, my solitude, my doubts and fears, my battle, and of course my animals.

Around the world, this house is as well known as I am. And people are still curious about it. Every summer, dozens of boats are parked along my private beach to try and catch a glimpse of me. Not a week goes by without people flocking together in front of my legendary blue gate, making this enormous piece of wood as famous as the Eiffel Tower. Some people even photograph themselves in front of it and send me the shot so I can autograph it. This place should become a museum after my passing, because it will respond to the needs of a very large public. It will not be a museum to glorify Brigitte Bardot, but a museum that will look like me, one that will look back on my human life and my animal dream. My last wishes are already confirmed: everything will be left intact at La Madrague. My furniture will remain where it is, and my installations, objects, and knickknacks will continue to populate my universe. In this way, my interior and my way of life will be offered to curious eyes. But for once, the idolatry I was the object of throughout my existence will be justified, because it will be for a good cause. This museum will offer regular funding to my foundation. Everything will be earmarked for the animals and their well-being. I embrace wholeheartedly the "place of pilgrimage" that La Madrague may become. Especially because I will not be resting far away from it. The formalities have been taken care of. A specific location has been accepted by the authorities, far from curious eyes, but near the graves in my little animal cemetery. I love the place I have chosen for my eternal rest; I selected it carefully. But since my decision, I no longer want to go there. A strange sensation seizes me when I think about it. I'm not really in a hurry; I'll have plenty of time to spend in that spot later.

This animal abnegation, before and after death, reinforces me each day. If my foundation was created through the sale of my most precious belongings and the gift of my properties, it is precisely so that my battle not die out with me. I struggle to imagine the Fondation Brigitte Bardot after me, even if I have done everything necessary by specifying that the organization remain in my image.

The power of my work must continue to shine as brilliantly as it did during my life. But there will be no more Brigitte Bardot. Her gall, her panache, her anger, her hard and gentle words will be no more. So who will actually replace me? My successors are already in place. And my natural heirs are everywhere in the world. They are all of you. You, who read my words and who have supported me with yours, your presence, your disciplined or complicated love, and with all of your testimonies that have supported me every day since my official declaration of war against animal cruelty. That love, which gives me stamina today, will be the strength of tomorrow. My energy will live on in one form or another. Because it is pure and selfless. I believe in the victory of Good. I believe in the victory of the Innocents. For "it is in the eyes of a dog that I saw the face of God."[16]

Sacrifice

Committing oneself to a cause means also forgetting oneself a little. Or a lot, in my case. One day, I broke with a life I was the center of to launch myself into an altruistic future. My daily life is the fruit of a long journey to reach it. Today, everything revolves around them, the animals, and not around me. It's about them, and that's it. This gives me a terrific force for my battle. Forgetting myself, though, can sometimes be a tricky business. I don't take care of myself at all, and I refuse to travel so I don't have to leave them, so I don't have to feel their absence. My hip problems, my little issues always come after them. I don't want to suffer, but my body doesn't interest me, and I am more attuned to their health and their pain than my own. Often, when we commit ourselves to a humanitarian act, like this one, we may also be doing it for ourselves, to maintain or

---

16 Quote from Éric-Emmanuel Schmitt, from his novel *Le Chien*, Albin Michel, 2012.

repackage our image. This notion is foreign to me. My life is them; my life belongs to them.

The animal cause, because it is founded on injustice and indifference, is worth our self-sacrifice. Quite often, it's a battle for life, a battle until death. And I admire martyrs. One of the films that has had the greatest impact on me is *Gorillas in the Mist*,[17] which examines the work of Dian Fossey with gorillas in the mountains of Africa. I never go to the movies, but my friend Jean-Louis Remilleux insisted that I see this film. At the screening, the French producers were waiting to hear my reaction: I was destroyed, I could no longer speak. Dian Fossey, activist; Dian Fossey, martyr; Dian Fossey, courageous; Dian Fossey, in love with gorillas, had singed me with a red-hot iron. Her story is extraordinary; it's the story of a saint. She is buried among the gorillas she loved so much.

A life of battle, ravaged by such violence, is unfortunately common. Dian Fossey disrupted poachers and the animal products industry. Joy Adamson's story is similar. This great lion protector was found dead on an African reserve in 1980. Her fatal wounds had been made to look as though she had been angrily clawed by the big cats, but in reality the only savages in this story were her human assassins. We must also remember Jill Phipps, another fighter in the field, who rebelled against the transportation of animals and revolted against this cruel industry that separates little calves from their mothers when they are barely eight days old before crowding them into trucks to languish on lethal factory farms. Jill, my sister in combat in the UK, succumbed in 1995, after being violently struck by a livestock convoy.

I also think about Barry Horne, chief of the English antivivisection commandos, who led an all-or-nothing movement to try and shake the

---

17 *Gorillas in the Mist: The Story of Dian Fossey*, directed by Michael Apted, 1988.

public from its lifeless slumber. Imprisoned and forgotten by everyone, he starved himself to death at the age of forty-two in 2001.

The elephants, too, have lost one of their greatest defenders. Wayne Lotter, a former ranger, was shot during an ambush in Tanzania in 2017. He had developed a program to reduce the massacre of elephants and created the PAMS Foundation to protect wildlife and fight against poaching and illegal trafficking.

With each of these deaths, it's almost as if another animal were being shot. It's an animal life that is disappearing, while no one moves a muscle. These martyrs' fights to the death should raise awareness, provoke worldwide homage, even adoration. No. We don't react. We prefer to tell ourselves that all of these people, sacrificed for animals, are crazy, lunatics, suicidal, extremists. Yes, they are extremists. But how can we not go to extremes when we are banging our heads so much against the wall of indifference? So we take action, again and again; we shout our words, louder and louder, and the words become sharper than before, hoping that one day we will touch the hearts of a handful of people. With these individuals, we are ultimately in the presence of heroes. The spinelessness of some humans is appalling.

The protection of animals is worth devoting our lives to. My life today is not worth very much because I am too old, and I don't know if I am cut from the same cloth as those heroes. Nevertheless, when I went out on the ice for the first time, I had written a will, because I knew I was risking my life. Several times over the course of recent years, I, too, have received death threats, but I couldn't care less. I told myself, "If I die, at least it's for a cause that I defended all the way to the end. And I will have given my life for that." If, one day, I had been offered a pact, saying, "Brigitte Bardot, give your life and we will never again kill horses for food," or, "We will no longer hunt wild animals," I would have knelt down and waited for my execution without any problem.

My words might sound shocking. But who today is actually listening to my supplications? Who out there would rather spread the word about the work of my foundation instead of controversies concerning me? Who screams in pain when they see human cruelty toward animals? In my former life, people prostrated themselves before me because I was beautiful, famous, in demand. Today, I bother people. I cannot explain the paralysis that has accompanied my rebellion. Either I no longer interest anyone, because the pretty legend rebelled too much, or I disturb people. Decision-makers, lobbyists, and politicians no longer want anything to do with me because I get them in trouble. They avoid me, and their silence is a refusal and an act of violence. People once spoke of our campaigns because they were the work of nice people who love nice animals. Today, we are millions of whistle-blowers against globalized cruelty. We continue forward, step by step, toward animal nonviolence. One day, we will no longer lock them up, one day we will no longer hunt them, one day we will no longer toy with them, one day we will no longer eat them. How much longer? No one knows. But the prisons unjustly incarcerating animals are rusty and outdated. The doors of awareness among the living are slowly opening. And I know that tomorrow I will no longer exist, but others will continue to push them open. I am closer to the end than to the beginning, and each day that passes is a respite and a hope: the hope that I have given life to a battle that is greater than my own existence. A battle that will not be abandoned after my disappearance. A vanguard that will endure after me. My death will give meaning to my life. My death will consecrate my battle and its meaning.

2

The Animal I Am

My Animal Instinct

As a child, I always knew I was an animal. With a nature that was at times sociable, other times solitary, I had a fierce temperament. Observing my surroundings from a distance, I despaired of finding anyone remotely like me. My bourgeois upbringing allowed me to integrate myself and adapt to polite society, but I rarely appreciated being in the company of other people for long periods of time. What I cherish most in human relationships is the naturalness that should come with them. This is rarely something I find, though. Superficial relationships in which we have to choose our words and find the best position from which to feel good about ourselves have never worked for me. I prefer sincerity. Pure and direct.

We are not taught to sniff. It is an animal gift and original instinct that I have been able to develop over the years. I probe and recognize a person immediately because I sniff them. My selective disposition prevents me from receiving any more than a few people to my home at La Madrague. The majority of my exchanges with my peers are done through letters. There are people who touch me deeply with a simple written note, and they become my friends by correspondence. Physical distance suits me quite well these days, even in the context of a great friendship. Meeting with people requires setting aside time and using verbal embellishments that are unnecessary when we interact on paper. I enjoy the basic, profoundly felt exchange: talking in order to actually say something. Today, even more than before, I am kissing proprieties and superficialities good-bye. I don't have any more time to waste on all of that.

This maladaptation to humanity, and the sheer dread that fills me when I am face-to-face with most humans, made me suffer atrociously during my life as an actress. I tremble before human beings who, in general, only define their connections with others through conflict, war, brawling, and vindication. This terror was even greater when I myself became the victim of power struggles. I can say this without shame: humans have hurt me. Deeply. And it is only with animals, with nature, that I found peace. My moments of quiet always found their raison d'être in the solitude of the countryside, far from any strangers, where I tucked myself away with the few people I trusted.

During the first part of my life, I never hid my temptation to drop everything and leave it behind. But I didn't know to what or to whom to turn. I knew that another life was possible—I loved and respected animals, and I felt and experienced an immeasurable well-being when I was near them—but it took me a while to transform this wonderful bond into a vocation.

For the filming of *The Night Heaven Fell* in 1957,[1] the whole team had moved into a small village in the south of Spain called Torremolinos, in Andalusia. One day, an apocalyptic storm ravaged the entire place: trees

---

1 French-Italian film directed by Roger Vadim and released in 1958.

were uprooted, homes destroyed, and the bodies of dead sheep were strewn along the beach. After the tornado, I welcomed a small donkey and a dog into my makeshift bedroom, which was nothing more than a room of whitewashed limestone. And I slept with this beautiful little group, safe and sound, for three nights. While my costars looked at me with wide eyes, I felt good, completely in step with who I was.

Since then, I have done everything possible to live surrounded by animals. I already had my dogs, who were waiting for me in my apartment in Paris, but each time I had to travel for work was a chance for another animal encounter. I tended to share my day-to-day life with animals. And after a while, we were no longer apart from one another at all. Today, I wake up, live, and sleep with my dogs. Their baskets are placed on either side of my bed, except for little Fripouille, who only appreciates the comfort of sleeping in my sheets . . . between my husband, Bernard, and me. She cohabitates very intelligently with the cats, who have also found their place on our bed. As a result, I can't stretch out my legs. This is the price I pay for everyone to get along. Bernard has had to accept living constantly with my companions. All the men in my life have adhered to this lifestyle. And those who were bothered by it packed their bags. And it was better that way.

Living with animals is to me a kind of mothering. I feel responsible for their well-being and their health. I can always sniff out their suffering from afar, and I know them so well that I'm never wrong. I know about my dogs' ill health before my own veterinarian does. The staff at La Garrigue takes care of my farm animals all day, until evening, when I visit to pet them and give them something to eat. I perceive instantly the state of their physical and mental health. When a goose is sick, I know it. Even if my caretaker insists that she is doing very well. The bond I form with my animals is innate. I feel like an animal because I live in total symbiosis with them. My reactions are more animal than human.

My Animal Nature

I have learned to live in simplicity and austerity; I don't know where it comes from. Certainly not from my upbringing. Maman was a very elegant woman; if she saw me walking barefoot, she would erupt in a fit of rage. Materialism is a concept that was always foreign to me, though. And if I carried an ounce of it in me, it was rapidly annihilated when I gave up everything for the animal cause. This is what made me give up my own interests once and for all.

Dispersing my belongings, giving away my houses, and selling a part of my life in the form of my keepsakes was not easy, of course. It is always a sacrifice to separate ourselves from the things that represent a part of us. Everything I sold came either from my grandparents, my parents, people who were in love with me, or people who cared about me. All of these objects I released contained my history, but also my utmost intimacy: objects, jewelry, souvenirs from films, costumes . . . I separated myself from them with a little heartbreak, but I told myself that all of these things were still only objects. Memories are located in the heart, not in the folds of a piece of fabric or the wood of a table. So I let go of all these pieces of my life, because I had the internal conviction that each one of them would help save animals. And I began to watch them leave with happiness. Animal life is much more important than the possession of beautiful jewelry in a safe, or luxurious cloth in a trunk.

And the older I became, the more simply I lived, with only the essentials, disregarding what was superfluous. Even in the greatest wealth, "having" never interested me. I was never attracted by luxury, high cost, or jewels. All of that was a means, never an end.

My Solitary Soul

Today, I live well. I am happy that I no longer have to waste my time speaking without saying anything. I do things that are natural and important to me, and I save my energy for this fight instead of spreading myself over so many nutty preoccupations.

My rhythm is nearly identical from one day to the next. I am more of a night person. I get up around nine o'clock, sometimes a bit before. I give my dogs something to eat, I call the two hundred pigeons who live freely at La Madrague, and I give them seeds. Then, I eat breakfast with Bernard, a breakfast we share with our dogs, of course. I read the newspapers, and I call my foundation and start dealing with pressing matters and emails. And then I leave for La Garrigue. I say hello to all my farm animals, and I get to work. I open my mail: a hundred letters a day from all over the world. I read every one and always respond to those that particularly touch me. The nature of these letters is quite varied: there are testimonies, cries of anger, requests for autographed photos, letters of friendship. I always give first priority to letters from people who are sick or old, and to those from children. Always the children. We must answer and speak to children. Young women write to me, too, not sure which direction to go in their lives. They are lost, heartbroken, they don't like their jobs, they're overwhelmed by their children. And then, of course, there are the people who have lost their animal and don't know who else to turn to because the pain of grieving an animal is unknown and misunderstood in our society. I cannot, in my soul and conscience, refuse the hand that reaches out for me in each letter. As much as possible, I offer support, help, a little note. A little note from me brings unimaginable joy to many of my correspondents, even if I can't resolve their problems. When someone calls me to help them, I feel like I have to complete a mission. And if I do nothing, I can't sleep. Something feels wrong; I feel guilty.

My age has not offered me an extra degree of philanthropy. I was always generous. And yet, my parents were not charitable people in the way I am. They were more like social personalities who liked to be talked about in glowing tones. I never saw them show compassion to anyone in particular, and my own hypersensitivity was always dismissed as a sign of immaturity. As an actress, one day I received a letter from an old woman near Meaux who was suffering from throat cancer. I went to visit her in the hospital, and when she saw me, she fainted. The doctor reproached me for my spontaneity. After that, I went to see her every year. I would spend the day with her, I would take her to a restaurant. When she passed away, Suzon left me her wedding band. I still wear it on my finger today.

The Choice to Survive

Animals and the choice I made to live with them and for them have been my guarantee of survival. My love for them gave me back my desire for life. My relationships with my dogs, cats, sheep, horses, seals, boars, wolves, and all the rest are natural and true, deeply true. They love me, I love them, and that's all.

They couldn't care less about B.B.

With them, I found a direction for my life, and life in general: this is how I found fulfillment. Cinema was just a stepping-stone; I never loved it. In the beginning, I enjoyed having people talking about me, but very quickly, it suffocated and destroyed me. Throughout my twenty years starring in movies, each time filming began, I would break out with herpes. A simple scene reading would upset me, as if I were a small child being brought to school. I dreaded it, going reluctantly because I thought it was all so pointless. Why should I put myself through so much just to play a role, if everything is fake, everything people say is fake, and if even the scenery is fake? I had a visceral need to do things that felt real.

Looking back, I believe that my two existences have complemented each other. I did, after all, enjoy living as an artist; as a star, I lived something exceptional, and I don't deny this, but the second era has added something to the first. The second chapter has put the finishing touches on the one that came before. Most of the things I learned before 1973 helped me later in my defense of animals. I was able to make a very clear parallel between human baseness and animal nobility. I was able to experience both human grandeur and smallness each day, sometimes—because of my status as a star—at an extreme level. I experienced mediocrity, pettiness, gestures of unmeasured adoration, hypocrisy, cowardice, and betrayal. The artificial domain in which I lived probably encompassed all sorts of weaknesses that I may not have encountered in a more anonymous life. Today, I wonder, though, if there is any domain that truly escapes superficiality. I fear I do not have the answer to this question.

So, when I take stock of it all, I can say that my earlier success in life did not make me happy. This constant blinding light never suited me. The only exposure I like, and have always liked, is the one I enjoy from my terrace at La Madrague. From high on the balcony bathed in sun, I observe the fluctuations of the Mediterranean in every season. Each morning when a flock of pigeons comes to peck at the seeds I hold out for them, and I am still given the ability to observe, every day, the beauty of nature, I cannot possibly doubt my decision.

Fame and Consequences

Light attracts us in a way nothing else does; we always dream about seeing something that shines, that seems inaccessible. We are fascinated by success and worldwide popularity. All my life, I was adored and idolized, and, in return, criticized and besmirched. People said things about me that were totally erroneous, and unfounded rumors took root. And when people ran out of things to say, they simply invented more.

I understand that my image has benefited from a certain improvement over the last fifteen years. I cite as evidence the many well-wishes I received on my eightieth birthday. This very clear change in public opinion took place because of what I have done for animals.

My life today is the one I always aspired to have. My solitary everyday life, surrounded by my husband and my animals, seems to be only fitting after decades of overexposure. For the days that are still granted to me, I have given myself over to patience and love, silence and tranquility.

The glorification of my life as a star, the violent reactions to my status as a protector of animals, and the total rejection of my positions and my forthrightness: these are some of the images that remain tattooed on my skin, sometimes as though they have been burned into me.

Living Myth

Being a public persona is a responsibility in and of itself, but being a "living myth" is quite another. And even though this label always had a way of making me run away, I am aware that even the mention of my name unleashes all kinds of passions.

Until today, I was the most photographed woman in the world, but my image has always gone beyond my actual person, a person who has been dragged through the mud on numerous occasions. What a paradox: a luminous and sunny icon and a stormy and shadowy individual!

During my life as an actress, I was pursued by paparazzi and held hostage by every horrible thing that could be said about a person. My reputation was sullied, and I was accused of a whole series of things I had never done. I made every effort in the world to have a normal life and to maintain healthy relationships, but love never mixes well with fame.

And many men didn't know how to separate the love they felt for me from what I represented in the eyes of the world.

Over and over, and especially in my two autobiographies, *Initiales B.B.* and *Pluto's Square*, I tried to quell any desire my readers might have had to become a star. As a result of the violence I experienced, the insults, the high-speed chases with journalists, and the bottle of sleeping pills constantly on hand to help me escape all of this, I know what it feels like to be hunted. I know how the relentlessly pursued animal feels: the turtledove shot midflight, the lion we put in a cage, the elephant we force to climb onto a ball to amuse children.

This harassment helped me cultivate an infallible instinct. I would sometimes be walking with my friend Jicky, whom I considered to be the brother I never had, when suddenly I would jump: "Don't move," I'd tell him, "there's a photographer . . ."

Jicky would be amused by my panic: "Listen, stop it, you're getting obsessive."

And then a camera lens would emerge a few minutes later from a bush or behind a trash can. I could sense their presence, the watching, the intention of the voyeur. I truly honed this sense of intuition during my relationship with Sami Frey, whom I consider one of the greatest loves of my life. The experience of being permanently observed and dissected was probably what defeated our love. We had no way to live normally and were forced to hide away, secluded, only going out at night, disguising ourselves, never going anywhere together, or else leaving one after the other. The first person would leave on reconnaissance and call the other: "Go ahead, it's okay, nobody's there." It was horrendous. No love could stand up to that, none. We couldn't stay at my apartment on Avenue Paul-Doumer, because I was in the middle of my divorce from Jacques Charrier, so Sami had rented a dive in someone's backyard that was equipped with a kind of storage room that we used as a bathroom. And we lived there, shut away in this burrow where no one would have thought of coming to drive us out. We barely had what we needed to make coffee, and we ate sandwiches that Sami bought wherever he could. Who could have imagined that at the very moment when *The Truth* was about to premiere,[2] a moment when I was such a star, I would be leading this kind of life? My life was horribly paradoxical. We were hiding like animals. Animals who were terribly in love and passionate, but fighting against the world.

When I left the world of cinema, I couldn't stand it anymore. The other side of the stardom coin was too heavy a burden to carry. Popularity is a poison. It kept me from living my life. I don't know what it means to sit quietly in a bistro, on a terrace, or in the theater without being approached by someone. I have only experienced this twice, and everyone was hanging on my every movement. I couldn't go to the movies, go grocery shopping, or walk through stores. To a lesser degree, this is still true today. When I leave La Madrague to go to my little farm at La Garrigue, I sometimes meet walkers or people driving who stop my car. Other times, Bernard will suggest going to have dinner in a small restaurant outside Saint-Tropez. I usually refuse because I know that people will come up to me, that they'll be watching what Brigitte Bardot is eating, how she holds her fork. They will ask for yet another photo or have me sign the restaurant's guestbook. And I will not refuse. Because I have never refused. This kind of thing is normal, and I accept it. People live and do what they feel like doing, and I accept it all the more because they are not aggressive, and even loving and tender toward me. But I still can't stand being watched, being examined, and being photographed. I'm tired of it all. Certain people are more fanatic than others: they want to embrace me, to touch me and rest their bulging and beseeching eyes on

---

2 *The Truth* is a French-Italian film directed by Henri-Georges Clouzot, released in 1960.

me. I have never understood—or at least always rejected—the idea of being an idol.

What is more, I still haven't quite grasped the reasons why I am seen as an icon. I have lived the way I wanted to live. I battled for my own freedom as a woman. That's all. Cocteau said I "lived like everyone while being unlike anyone." The secret probably lies in this nuance. My gestures and actions were either adored or hated; there was no in-between. As soon as I did something people didn't like, it would take on huge significance, and everything would be exaggerated to unimaginable proportions. This was probably because of my frank and, at times, impulsive and uncompromising nature. I also know that some people really wanted to hurt me. There was a kind of jealousy. Perhaps because I had succeeded in a somewhat magical way? The fact that I came from a bourgeois and well-off family, breaking with the traditional image of the artist, probably also has something to do with it. I benefited from incredible luck and quickly became a phenomenon, without ever having to pull strings. And when I did express myself, I'm sure my nonchalant tone angered more than one person. Especially because I always felt free to say that I didn't like the lot I'd been given in life; this was an offense to many people. It was true, though: I was not even twenty-five years old and I was already declaring loud and clear that I would do anything in the world if it would make people stop talking about me. I condemned the golden prison I was locked inside. I know very well that this might sound like a provocation, but I couldn't pretend.

Something Madame de Staël said summarizes very well the torment that being famous can foster: "Glory is the dazzling death of happiness." I am convinced that celebrity is destructive. One has only to look at the lives of Marilyn Monroe, Romy Schneider, or even Marlene Dietrich, who died alone in her apartment on Avenue Montaigne. I also think of Annie Girardot, who left this world suffering and forgotten by everyone.

The majority of great actresses met tragic ends. When I said good-bye to this job, to this life of opulence and glitter, images and adoration, the quest to be desired, I was saving my life. Choosing animals tore me from the claws of a miserable future; I had found a direction for my life. Being a living myth is neither an occupation nor an end. It is an accident, a stroke of luck, a delicious but ephemeral pleasure. Discovering your reason for being brings you back to Earth and anchors you there. Fame is the illusion of power. Taking action gives you back your strength, however limited it may be. If there is any proof of glory's infertility, it can be seen in the animal cause I try so hard—sometimes in vain—to carry forward.

The Most Beautiful Woman in the World

I never felt beautiful. I am only now starting to understand the famous beauty at the root of my success. I grew up, lived, and matured in an abyss of self-doubt. Each time I had to go out, everything became a source of hesitation: how to dress, how to do my hair, how to hold myself, how to speak . . . I was always uncertain and unconvinced about the appearance I put forward. This probably comes from the fact that Maman stuck a dental apparatus on me for most of my childhood. This happened to go very well with my huge glasses and dreadful hairstyle: I had been saddled with a perm that was far too frizzy in an attempt to banish my natural hair, which was "straight as a baguette." I hated the way I looked so much that when I was ten or eleven, I decided to own my ugliness. I told myself: "I'm ugly, my life won't be easy, so I just need to accept it." And this stayed with me.

This may sound astonishing, but I do not at all have confidence in myself. Everything frightens me. The amount of strength I have to display in order to combat this defect is superhuman. The idea of making a move or having to confront someone terrifies me. When I decide or agree to do something, I am sure of myself, but the moment of putting it into action is an ordeal. I am always afraid that I won't reach my goal. When I am forced to enter into a relationship with third parties, doubt always makes me stumble. Human nature intimidates me: I'm frightened of not being understood, of not being able to get my ideas across. This is particularly the case today when an animal's life is at stake. When I involve myself personally, I'm never calm. When I start something that ends in failure, I blame myself; it hurts me and feeds my lack of self-assurance.

As a child, in addition to finding my physical body deplorable, I was also terribly withdrawn. I was not good in school, and my parents were not very proud of me. Only classical dance liberated me from these complexes. When I would face the mirror and perform a few steps, the elegance of the movement reflected back to me a pleasing image. I could have been a dancer, and I think I would have loved it. It was very difficult, but each rehearsal was a victory over myself. I had no other choice but to get beyond my own self-doubt. The rigor and endurance that are inherent in the classical world have left indelible traces on my temperament. I am still very disciplined, I always finish what I begin, and I never do things halfway. My way of standing, sitting, and moving, even with my crutches, is a legacy of those hours of dance, the battle I led with and against myself.

Publicity

One of the most prevalent accusations I face in my life of combat is that I have used animal suffering to improve my image. During numerous interviews, as if protecting animals wasn't a worthy cause in and of itself, I have been asked about the benefits it held for my career. Even in 1962, eleven years before I left film and at the height of my stardom, journalist Pierre Desgraupes asked me on *Cinq colonnes à la une* if my plea for the animals in the slaughterhouse was intended to be a promotional stunt. I replied that I was probably the only person in the world who didn't need publicity. In reality, the only thing that needed it was the cause I was starting to tackle. And I was ready to offer it all of my own renown.

A few years later, in 1976, Jacques Chancel invited me on his *Radioscopie* show, during which I had the insolence to compare the birth of my young animal organization to a crusade. Despite his recognized talent, the journalist was quick to echo the suspicions shared by many of his colleagues. Did I love animals more than people? Why didn't I want to use my immense popularity in the service of greater tragedies like world hunger, needy children, the elderly, or the unemployed? I had been brought up a certain way and was extremely perceptive, so I quickly swept away these objections and stood my ground. All humanist and humanitarian causes already had their defenders; animals were sorely lacking them. Only the SPA, the Bird Protection League (LPO), the Wild Animal Protection League (ASPAS), and the Aid to Animals in Abattoirs (OABA) were leading the fight. Considering that the suffering of animals was ignored or discounted by the great majority, I wanted to fill this void.

Nevertheless, publicity was never a stranger. Because I did go looking for it. More than once. I sold myself to make people buy what I was selling. But for a good cause! To pay for my foundation and to help animals, I agreed to promote an English aftershave and to represent French products like wine and honey in the United States.

Making animal life respected on Earth was my only motivation. And it took me time, obstinacy, and courage to make people understand. The worst period of my life as far as criticism and outpourings of hatred is still my journey onto the ice to stop the massacre of baby seals in 1977.

As I described in the first chapter, I was worse than ridiculed there and found myself engaging in trench warfare against the Canadian and Norwegian press, who had come to plead for the sealskin industry. I was asked if I ate steak and was told my coat contained the skin of a *blanchon*, even though it was made of brown fluff. I was told that Valéry Giscard d'Estaing, who had supported me by banning the importation of sealskin in France, was himself a habitual hunter. Up against a wall, I fired a death blow at this hostile audience by saying that in Europe we called them "Canadian murderers."

Less predictably, French journalists from *L'Aurore* and *Le Figaro* were also very hostile toward me in Canada. I met one *Figaro* journalist by the name of Desjardins. He maintained that Valéry Giscard d'Estaing was only taking part in my battle to keep his electoral votes. He told me that my public speaking engagements were bordering on insanity and that the Canadian government should have had me thrown out *manu militari*, because to him it was unthinkable that a foreigner would come to a country to call its people assassins. Not stopping there, he said I was a terrible actress and that my press conferences had proven it once more. I ended this indictment by openly informing him that unlike him, "I had balls." I think he probably still remembers that. Interestingly enough, later on, Desjardins radically changed his opinion and even asked to accompany me on my second campaign to Canada in 2006.

When I left Canada, I wept tears of blood. I did not suspect that the worst was yet to come. In France, the newspapers had banded together to taunt me. Tired, hopeless, and disgusted to see a battle for animal life and justice sullied to this point, I returned to my Paris apartment on Boulevard Lannes. On the table, I discovered an entire series of terrible newspaper cuttings. In one filthy rag of a paper, Philippe Bouvard explained that the seal massacre had been a publicity stunt to boost my low popularity. Added to this were comments from people close to me:

from Madame Renée, my housekeeper, who said, "We're not proud of you in the building," and even my own mother, contaminated by the aggression toward me that was all around, who felt "ashamed." And finally, to top it all off, even in Saint-Tropez I was laughed at: I stank of fish, I had grown a seal-whisker mustache, my own fur must already be going white. Those were just a few. I nevertheless want to specify that, like some of his colleagues, Philippe Bouvard later changed his position, too, and even confessed one day that he had been wrong about me and since then has christened me his "best enemy." After a while, time heals things and people change their minds.

But the memory of this injustice and this gratuitous nastiness in response to a humanist battle were still carved into me. Humanity disgusted me. True friends like Allain Bougrain-Dubourg and Franz Weber supported me emotionally during this period. I needed time to get past the hatred I had fallen victim to, and to be capable of seeing that not everyone thought that way. As news of my trip and the image of Brigitte Bardot hugging a baby seal made their way around the world, a movement of popular support was born. And I drew from it the strength to fight. In my most private memories, I still hold onto the gestures of friendship and gratitude I received from millions of unidentified people. Several decades before the advent of social networks, public expression was open only to certain people. It was therefore difficult to evaluate how the public felt about one event or another. The thousands of letters I received at that time, though, told me I was right: in people's hearts, my trip onto the ice was widely commended, so much so that a nickname had been given to me, like a new birth, a new identity: B.B. *Phoques*. B.B. Seals.

Humanizing Animals

Yet another faulty reflex. Humanizing animals, or animalizing humans, is a false debate. And besides, what difference is there? My idea of respecting the lives of everyone means that I consider the nonhuman animal the equal of the human animal. The love I wish to bring to vulnerable beings does not take into account the differences between species. Compassion has no boundaries. It is not "humanizing" them to say that wild, domestic, and marine animals have basic needs. Life is sacred, and it is imperative to do everything to preserve, respect, and protect it in every area. I also use the same language when I speak about all representatives of a species. For me, the cries of pain in experimental laboratories are not "vocalizations," as we might read in certain scientific summaries. Animal beings are not numbers. Slaughtering, to me, is similar to extermination. Bullfighting is a sentence to public execution coupled with a torture session, and filet mignon is nothing but a piece of cadaver under cellophane.

To say that we must take care of humans before animals seems like a lazy attempt to release us from guilt. The animal cause is a humanitarian cause, that of defending the weak, the oppressed, and the humiliated. Finally, let us consider this possibility: What if adding a few words onto "animal," making it "an animal being" and recognizing our common biology, could turn the historic and irreversible shame of how we have treated them totally on its head?

Misanthrope

Another thing people say about me is that I prefer animals to people. In many respects, and theoretically, I would say YES! But things are not so simple. Fighting for animal protection is often seen as something for people on the margins: grass-eaters, lunatics, ultrasensitive people, and people who are disconnected from (real) problems in society. There are several explanations for this: the first is that taking care of animals requires that we take a bit of distance from the oversize ego of men, and *that* does not go down easy. The world is organized to exist for and remain at the service of the human being. As a result, even virtue must support his interests. Altruism and benevolence have no value unless they are a vehicle for his own gain. Gratuitous generosity, or generosity freely offered to a species other than his own is out of the question. When we save a human, we are heroes. When we save an animal, what are we? Taking care of animals also calls into question a belief held by (almost) everyone: that they live to be at our service. Imagining them as something other than our resources would be broadening our "anthropocentric" horizons, in other words, viewing reality through a lens other than the human eye. It would no longer be a question of exploiting nature, but of living *with* it. And sometimes submitting to it.

Being sensitive to animals does not make me insensitive toward human beings. I can sniff out very quickly if my peers are experiencing distress, if they need to interact or be reassured. Everywhere in the world, there are beings who need to be loved but have no one to give them any love. Taking an interest in animals does not turn away the attention I owe to my fellow beings as a human and a woman. On the contrary, in 2001, I made the trip to Bucharest with my foundation for a stray dog sterilization campaign. Fortunately, this journey also allowed me to visit and bring needed support to several orphanages and retirement homes in Romania.

If I or my foundation takes care of people in need, the elderly, the sick, or people who are needy, elderly, sick, or simply dependent on others, it is in a more personal context. Apart from Franck, my secretary, who carries out all of my requests, no one is told about these kinds of things. When I read here and there that B.B. doesn't take care of anyone but animals, I feel no need to reestablish certain truths, because it's no one else's business. I am very careful not to subscribe to what I think is a vulgar attitude: flaunting the help we lavish on other people. My generosity is known by the women and men who can see and hear it with their hearts, and who can benefit from it.

Unfit Mother

As I've said before, when I worked in film, I was called a whore, a slut, a bad actress, and more. I remember distinctly the pathetic impression of humanity that was formed in my mind the day I gave birth by myself in my home. The fact that I was hunted even on the day I had a baby caused me irremediable trauma. It was awful; I have never experienced anything worse. When a woman gives birth, the balance between the outpouring of her body and the preservation of a certain modesty is difficult to maintain. In my case, everything was tainted. I was giving life to something and was forced to share this moment with the whole world because hundreds of photographers had congregated beneath my windows. The delivery room had been set up in my house; I had no operating room. Only the minimum of what was medically necessary had been brought, and I can't imagine what would have been done if something had gone wrong. This moment was a shock, a wound, a tearing. I was no longer myself, I no longer belonged to myself. And Nicolas is the one who bore the consequences of this. Looking back, I know that, emotionally and psychologically, I associated his birth with this trauma. I could not face and take ownership of my pregnancy and his birth because I was too young, too inexperienced, too active, too well-known, too unstable. I was, unfortunately, too normal in an abnormal life. A woman should never be forced to have a child, even if love comes with time, because this event should be a happy one. And if it is not, it scars you for life. This was the case for me. That moment, the nervous animal twisting in pain on her delivery bed, greatly damaged things in my life.

When my memoirs came out, I was slammed for having stated that I would have preferred "giving birth to a puppy instead of a human." These harsh and crude words only betray my inability, my unsuitability, my ignorance of the very language needed to describe this situation. This was not an insult directed at my son—my God, no—but rather at the pain I felt at the absence of this maternal feeling. Maternal instinct is learned, with time and in a peaceful life, both of which I was deprived of. I still live with this rift today.

During Nicolas's childhood, our interactions were difficult. For both of us. And then things settled down. Today we call each other regularly. He lives in Norway and visits me once a year at La Madrague, either by himself or accompanied by his family: his wife, my granddaughters, and even my great-granddaughter. Our relationship has normalized itself. My son is wonderful, and I love him in a very special way. As he does me. He does not resemble me very much, though. Physically, he inherited a great deal from his father. His facial expressions, his gestures, and his way of speaking are very "Charrier."

Nicolas doesn't seem to hold a grudge against me, nor does he seem to have any bitterness about the strange kind of mother I was. He is not spiteful. He did suffer, though. I don't know if he learned things from me, from our shared history. We have never spoken about his childhood. Ever. And I think it's useless to go back and talk about the past: it's over. Besides, when we do spend a little time together, we speak very little as it is. He comes to see me, and we live side by side. It's a relationship I'm not sure how to define. I don't tell him anything really significant; I don't even know if he likes it at my house. And I wouldn't ask him. This is not a question I can ask him. Maybe one day, something will come from his side. But only from him. I shouldn't beg for words, gestures, or attention. I can't do that. Nicolas is filled with great strength, character, and intelligence. He knew how to form a cocoon, a family.

In spite of all of this, I enjoy a special relationship with my granddaughter, Théa. She is very interested in me and in my past. One year, she came to visit me, and we had a hard time understanding each other between Norwegian, English, and French. The following summer, she returned wearing a Vichy dress and speaking in a French she had been perfecting over many months. I believe she did it for me. For her grandmother. I am infinitely grateful to her for that.

Controversies

My sincerity and my desire to go all the way have often given me setbacks. And yet, in spite of my great lack of self-confidence, I never regret anything. I never turn back to the past. My various charges of "inciting racial hatred" annoyed me, but they did not affect me.[3] I never asked anyone to be a racist and I don't think I have fed racial hatred. What hurt me most was one journalist's suggestion that my extreme opinions "had not helped the animal cause." I reject this hurtful accusation, which is unfounded and unfair.

I had already been criticizing ritual kosher and halal slaughter for fifteen years before my trial, as well as the horrifying and unregulated ritual sacrifices that take place during the "celebration" of Eid-al-Kebir. I had spoken out against these things for one reason only: the throats of

---

3 Brigitte Bardot has been convicted five times. In 1997 and 1998: following the publication of an editorial in Le Figaro, April 26, 1996; in 2000: following the republication of a letter from the appendix of the second volume of her memoirs, Pluto's Square, in 1999; in 2004: following the publication of A Cry In the Silence (Ed. du Rocher, 2003); and in 2008: following the publication of a letter to President Sarkozy in Info Journal, no. 59, dated October 31, 2006.

animals are slit open without any prior stunning, leaving us to imagine the agony they endure. They struggle and scream, emptying themselves of their blood. Our resistance movements through the foundation, our demonstrations, and our petitions had never changed anything. And suddenly, one so-called "*Cocorico* nationalist" letter stirred up a hornet's nest. "*Mon cri de colère*" appeared in *Le Figaro* on April 26, 1996, and openly criticized the Eid sacrifices and the cropping up of clandestine slaughterhouses. I was even angrier because, shortly afterward, the prefecture authorized cutting the throats of one thousand sheep near my home in Bazoches. I viewed this gesture as a provocation. I was charged on December 19, 1996, released for a first offense but convicted on appeal.

I can understand if the stances I have taken have sometimes interfered with the humanist message I carried, but I don't regret it. What matters to me is that I denounced the horror and the suffering of cutting living animals' throats.

The idea is not to forbid religious activities, but the cruelty that follows from them. The problem in France is that people completely bypass the law of 1962—which obliges us to only open the throat of an *unconscious* animal—through the use of convenient exemptions. This is the real problem for me, and I will return to it in the passages of this text dedicated to it.[4]

Every year since then, when the calendar indicates that the Eid holiday is beginning—along with its droves of legal and clandestine throat-slittings—my sense of powerlessness is at its peak. My desolation, my pain, and my distress join with those millions of creatures who are cut open in atrocious suffering. And all of this with the complicity of my country's government. I can't stand it. We cannot continue to accept in

---

4 Chapter 3, in the sections about Religion and Tradition.

this day and age that religious traditions express themselves through animal sacrifice.

I have a short fuse when it comes to these massacres. I don't wish harm on anyone, but I want rules, not injustice. Would I be so focused on some believer's lifestyle if I didn't have to condemn the cruelty of ritual slaughter in slaughterhouses? Certainly not. But I cannot keep quiet in front of atrocities: they go against every fiber of my being, and my anger is too powerful.

The truth is that I have always been wary of religion whenever it dominates human thoughts and actions. I wrote a letter one day because a woman in Nigeria was supposed to be stoned to death, and she was pardoned. I fight against cruelty, brutality, and the exploitation of the weakest, especially when this is done in the name of God, and I denounce lifestyles and pretenses that devalue humans and deny them free will. Religion that subjugates, that is practiced with one's eyes closed, and extremism that makes people commit terrible acts: I denounce these things, as well. The last reason for my lack of regret concerning the statements I made is that they led a great number of French people to stop and think about ritual slaughter. I bombarded people and politicians to such an extent about the cruelty of these practices that eventually everyone started talking about it. Yes, I may have sacrificed my image a bit. Too bad. And all the better for the animals.

Following that initial conviction, I was immediately labeled as a member of the Front National. But the origins of this label go back further. It first started in June 1991, when my foundation had me participate in a questionnaire about Eid for *Présent*. I had been told ahead of time that it was a politically "far-right" newspaper, but I didn't pay attention. Having never participated in politics in my life, I simply didn't know what the "far right" was. All I can say is that if *L'Humanité* had sent me the same questionnaire, my responses would have been the same. The article created a scandal, without my understanding why. And from that day on, I was considered a racist, a *frontiste*, a muse for Jean-Marie Le Pen, and more. And to make matters worse, one year later, I met Bernard d'Ormale, my future husband and a friend of Jany, the wife of Jean-Marie Le Pen. My Bernard was never an adviser to Le Pen, much less his éminence grise, as was often written.

Impulsive

Perhaps people sometimes have a hard time understanding me because I am impulsive. I am straightforward, and that frightens people. When an animal is lying on the ground, my anger is volcanic, my outrage knows no obstacles and sweeps away everything in its path: morality, decorum, right-mindedness. I get carried away. I have always been this way. Fortunately or unfortunately, I'm not sure which, it made me the passionate person I am.

In 1953, Julius and Ethel Rosenberg were sentenced to death in the electric chair. They were accused by the US government of spying for the USSR. I had just married Vadim; I was still a bit childish but already antiauthority. In spite of the tidal wave of protest around the world, nothing seemed to be able to prevent this death sentence from being carried out. So one night, I decided to write messages on piles of small scraps of paper: Free the Rosenbergs! Save them! Shame on the United States! And I asked Vadim to bring me onto Route d'Orly so I could throw all of these little missives out the window, hoping to bring a little help to these people. I was so naive. The Rosenbergs were electrocuted a short time later.

Sometimes I think very little before I speak or act. The strict and bourgeois upbringing I had received was founded on control, but this never kept me from saying what I was thinking. I never bite my tongue, and I am not familiar with the frustration of silence. I am also capable of making a decision in a matter of seconds, as I did during the sale of my apartment on Boulevard Lannes. Dalida had visited it, and my housekeeper informed me that the singer had come dressed in an extraordinary coat; very *snob*, very chic . . . but fur. I called the real estate agency to tell them I would never let Dalida have the apartment, despite all of the affection I felt for her.

I assume responsibility for this impulsivity, these outbursts. Because without this rage, my battle would not have become what it is today. In September 1981, I learned that a florist in Saint-Tropez had killed her cat by beating him with a stick. The night it happened, her neighbors had heard the poor animal's screams for hours, as well as the wrath of the woman and her son, an accomplice in the crime. I had known this woman for twenty years, not one or two, so I went into her shop and demanded that she explain her crime. She threw me out, ordering me to mind my own business. Without realizing it, she had confirmed to me the terrible torture that cat had endured. Furious, I began screaming in the public square: "*Salope! Salope! Salope!*" The florist took me to court for defamation and indecency. I was charged but won the case a year later.

My emotions are sometimes too excessive, but I never regret this. I would rather be like this than be indifferent. Sometimes I seriously lack diplomacy, I know.

Loves, Etc.

Fervor controls my life, and my feelings most of all. Love as such is worth nothing if it is not passionate. I love love, which is exactly the reason I was often unfaithful. In every relationship, I would always run off in search of other loves when the present one became a little lukewarm. I don't like the in-between, the not-as-good. I have always sought out passion, and, whenever it reached its end, I would pack my bags. Love, lived in an innate and instinctive way, has always guided my steps, my days and nights. As I have often said, friendship is loose change when compared to passionate love. This is why I have never tried to maintain relationships with the few men I was madly in love with. Things happened differently with Serge Gainsbourg. For one thing, our idyll was very short, and what was more, at the end of his life, we were back in consistent contact by telephone. He felt alone, very unwell, and very unhappy. And I also was alone, and I also was very unhappy. In spite of the years that had passed since our liaison, an extraordinary complicity remained between us. I think our meteoric passion, which ended up not lasting very long, had transformed and taken on the shape of a relationship between two old people! So I accompanied Serge, and he accompanied me. It was a kind of fidelity between two creatures who were not as wild as before, but who could still recognize each other in a single glance. Serge is a special case, though, because love until death, symbiotic love, the unique and unspeakable love I shared with two other men, never earned this kind of continuation. I couldn't do it; I loved Sami too much, and I loved Jean-Louis Trintignant too much, to have friendly relationships with them. And I don't think that either one of them would ever come running to me looking to be rescued, any more than I would go looking for help from them. And yet absolute love, love that is full and whole and self-sufficient, and which I felt for those two exceptional people, is part of the most beautiful pages of my life. Yes, these relationships inhabit a past that is long gone, but they carry within them, because of their unique intensity, the grace of eternity.

I am adamant when I say that I feel more animal than human. I have the appearance of a human being, so I have the flaws of a human being, but inside, I am an animal being. I need freedom and protection at the same time, and the person who lives with me must take this balance into account. I have an immense need for independence, but no need for soli-tude. Like an animal, I cannot stand being abandoned and left alone when I have offered my love. I am aware that I have this dog-like side, this desire to protect my house, to guard my temple, this need for tenderness, affec-tion, human warmth, and freedom. There is nothing I detest more than small talk and people getting together for soirees. As an actress, I was mis-erable whenever I was required to attend these kinds of events. Each time I was forced to go was horrible for me. I did it halfheartedly and would impatiently wait for the end. I thought only of taking shelter at Bazoches, where I lived like a wild child with my hair undone, feet bare or in rubber boots, wearing jeans, huge puffy jackets, and in my natural state.

I am very fearful. I have always moved within a small circle. I like hav-ing long-lasting personal, friendly, and professional relationships with people. I think of my manager, Mama Olga, and my makeup artist, Odette, who was like a mother to me. I stood by her until her death, and I miss her a great deal. Franck, my personal secretary, has been close to me for decades. And I haven't even mentioned Bernard, whom I always knew would be my last husband. Bernard married my battle when he asked me to be his wife. Day after day, he fights alongside me, sharing his reflections and ideas about how to achieve my goals. Contrary to what has often been said, though, Bernard does not tell me how to think. In fact, he softens me quite a lot. When I met him, he offered me the pres-ence and comfort I had been missing for so long. In the seven years that preceded his coming into my life, I had suffered from a great solitude; I was overwhelmed with ordeals, and I thought I was too old to live with a companion. It was not for a lack of suitors, but none of them matched the lifestyle I had chosen. And then Bernard arrived. I liked him because he was himself, separate from me. He had his own personality, intelligence, erudition; he had a kind of insolence that amused me, and he has held onto it. Bernard had secured the very fragile target I had become.

Our daily life today is not mundane. We speak to each other very little, and our two autonomies cohabitate in relative harmony. Born on August 15, like Napoleon, Bernard can sometimes be very authoritarian, and I admit I am not very easy to live with, either. But we have been married for twenty-five years now, and when he leaves, even just for a day, I find it terribly difficult to live without him. I can't explain the permanence of this relationship, except by saying that Bernard is a man who has always known how to distinguish the glory I represent from the being I am. Bernard is not fooled by anything anyone else says, critics and admirers alike. He is one of the only people in my life who has continuously separated Brigitte from Bardot, and this brings me a belated but lifesaving solace.

3

My Animal Life

How Did Animals Save Me?

Life is not worth living unless it is nourished by love. Love is a motor, a source of hope, and a lifeboat. It was mine at a time when all I had left were questions without answers. Some may think I'm exaggerating when I say that animals saved me. But I will say it again: they *did* save me. They are capable of saving other humans, as well, and they might perhaps save all of humanity.

The love I feel for animals is always increasing. It is a boundless affection that I have never felt for a human. I never get tired of them, and they never disappoint me. Men and women are not always as remarkably beautiful on the outside and the inside as animals are. Animals give their hearts entirely and unconditionally. And they never ask for it back. Unlike people, animals only make me sad when they pass away. They have an extraordinary way of existing: they have nothing. They possess nothing apart from their life. And as companions, they entrust that life to you. This is why I developed such a great desire to protect them. I worry about them, I keep them company and reassure them when they wake up in the night, I talk to them when I sense they are feeling sad, and I care for them. I do with them what other people are able to do with the children of humans.

Animals saved me because what binds me to them is a love that is pure, felt, and lived. To live in contact with them is to live in the essence of life. Allowing yourself to exist in pretense is tiring after a while. Living in the spotlight with people watching and expecting things damages us on the inside. And to spend our days turned toward ourselves, toward what people might be saying about us, is very dangerous because then we forget what is true.

I was able to make it through my "Pluto's Square," the darkest period of my life, thanks to my animals. They were there when I was alone, they were there when I was sick, they were there when I was depressed. And it is truly only in their company that I was able to resist. Just like children I would have wanted to shelter from these circumstances, I was always concerned about protecting my animals. I had breast cancer, but my animals never sensed it because I never showed any signs of weakness. I didn't want to. As I have already said, flaunting one's physical suffering is, to me, a disgraceful and immodest thing to do.

Life is a miracle, and I have always been aware of this. So when evil reared its head, I was convinced that I was stronger than it. This was because I had the mindset, the force to conquer it. This is usually what carries me through: this power I have within me to face whatever is attacking me. I don't want to let myself be knocked down and I don't want anyone to know what I'm going through. Animals—dogs in particular—are very sensitive to moods, and their psyche must not be disturbed as this may upset them and leave them traumatized and stressed. I refused to do this. It is probably because of this constant effort not to rattle them psychologically, even when I was at my worst, that I was able to make it through these challenges. I didn't want to falter, for myself or for them. I held onto this discipline throughout my illness, as well as during my periods of depression and terrible emotional suffering—sometimes almost more than I could take.

I am a very internal person and can easily lose myself in chasms of thought. I have always wondered about things, asking myself questions about the meaning of life, good and evil, the necessary and the superficial. These metaphysical questions sometimes come upon me during difficult moments, like the loss of someone dear to me, heartbreak, or events related to animals. The annual Yulin massacres in China, which I will talk about later, and the celebration of Eid in France provoke an insane despair within me. These mass murders horrify me so much that they bring about dark periods of anguish in my life.

I experience everything on the inside. I have so many things bouncing around deep within me that if I were to release some of the steam one day, I would resemble a pressure cooker with a flowered chignon. In this regard, I have very few correspondents who are able to calm me down, few people I can put my trust in. Sometimes I would like to relieve myself of some of my torment, but most of the time my exchanges with others lack depth. This absence of mental reciprocity in conversations can make my daily life feel incomplete. It's not by accident that I fell head over heels for introverted men. This was an echo of my own need for innerness, even if that meant that the relationship took a rather tortured turn. Mirko had an inner fragility, and Sami and I we were folded in on each other; our world was impenetrable. Our two universes were connected, and no one could understand it. Life, of course, decided that this story was not going to continue; perhaps there was a negative energy in the fusion of our hearts, or perhaps our shuttered existence would have ended tragically.

My state of being is determined by events and encounters with others. These days, my vitality and my desires for lightness and fun are very often left unsatisfied. I rarely laugh. Most of the time, I work in my office. I am a witness to the horrors of the world, and this keeps me in a relatively morose state. I am still quite capable of laughing, though! The people who come to see me are, for the majority, involved in the animal cause. We share the same problems, and they often come to find consolation from me.

Quite happily, my window on the world remains the mail I receive, coming from men and women who tell me all the good I am doing for them. Their words of thanks soften my days in an incredible way. One day, I opened an envelope containing nothing but a large white page and a simple "I love you." I burst out laughing. Emotional and spiritual declarations of love offer a wonderful change of pace from my solitary existence.

Animals also have saved me because they keep me from being a complete prisoner of myself. I have just celebrated my eighty-third birthday, and this takes on no kind of importance for me. In fact, I hate September 28. Instead of being a joyful, convivial, pleasant day, it is a time when I am harassed, overwhelmed with mail, requests, and interviews. It's the worst time of the year for me, one during which I feel like disappearing from circulation. So many declarations of love; it's wonderful, but it's too much. As usual. My life can be summarized with those words: *too much*. It could be part of a slogan: *Bardot, c'est trop*. The anonymous well-wishes sent to me by the hundreds are often invasive and stifling. The day I turned eighty, for example, I received ten thousand letters all at once. For me, an ideal birthday would be a birthday that everyone forgot.

You cannot imagine how heavy a burden celebrity is to carry. I had fun with my own fame for the first few years, but it took on such a magnitude, beyond what anyone imagined. I am no longer popular, I am globalized. Everywhere in the world, wherever I go, I am known and recognized. It keeps me from living. The life I've had does not resemble the one I would have hoped for. I wanted to do things with passion, enthusiasm, and liberty. The result was that I had no liberty. I don't know what it's like to walk somewhere with no one watching you. I haven't experienced that in a very long time. Even today, each time I leave the house is an escapade. One of my last escapes was a trip to the dentist. He had so wisely set up his office near Place des Lices, the tourist heart of Saint-Tropez. It is so well located that I usually arrange to not have any tooth pain in the summer. When there are no tourists, the Tropéziens leave me alone. Well, if the painkillers aren't working and I have no other choice but to go see him, my caretaker drops me off outside, and from there I hurry on my crutches toward the door to the office. For the same reasons, I can never take a walk by the port. It's been ages since my arrival stopped provoking riots, but heads will still turn when I go by, though I did manage a very discreet visit to see the Sea Shepherd trimaran that had been named after me on my eightieth birthday. But as a general rule, I am worn out, exhausted by this circus. I am also unwilling to disguise myself to go somewhere incognito. I've never done that before. I couldn't; I always wanted to remain as I was. And strangely, even when I did wear headscarves or sunglasses, people still recognized me.

Sometimes I dream about being able to stroll around, look in shop windows, and choose a gift for myself or somebody else. Sometimes I also wish I could sit outside a little café, watch the *pétanque* players and the people passing, just to see people living their lives.

I don't mind the globalization of my image when it concerns animals, however. One might think that today, at my age, I would be spared some of the spotlight. But on the contrary: as the "Animal Fairy," people worship me with an extraordinary admiration that goes far beyond my career in film. It's as if I have been sanctified. I once received an unbelievable letter that caused me to weep, describing me as a saint, the Mother Teresa of animals, the modern Saint Francis of Assisi. In reality, all I did was give myself, to the detriment of what life could have given me—namely, an agreeable and pleasant situation in life, moments of relaxation, this or that. My rejection of all of this is what people praise me for.

So, I was wrong. I sincerely thought that by committing myself to animal protection, I would be able to return to anonymity. I told myself that the activism would merge with my person, that this cause would surpass me, myself, and my physique. Even though I was mistaken, when all is said and done, I have come out better for it. Sometimes people are pious toward me, they come close, wanting to touch me like a holy object. Though not a relic, I hope! And if my personal space is quasi-nonexistent, it is because of the emotional rapport I have always maintained with each and every person. People come toward me spontaneously, toward my authenticity, my natural manner, my welcome. One day, a lady with a bouquet of flowers was waiting on my doorstep, and I let her come in and visit my home. She left with the impression that she had been a part of my life for a few moments, that she had experienced a short instant of my private life. I also welcomed two young girls into my life one afternoon. They acted as though it were a miracle. And to me they brought a bit of fresh air, a stream of love and kindness. Doing these things for perfect strangers is a unique pleasure. My house is perhaps the only "star's house" in the world that is not monitored. I have a security guard, my dog Craquotte—who is ready to eat the buns off of any intruder—and that's it. I am protected by a small blue gate and by the decency of the people who love me and who don't dare cross certain limits.

Another time I was returning to La Madrague in my Renault 4 with my dogs when I was forced to stop in the middle of the road to avoid a running dog. A couple in their sixties were trying to catch her. When the woman recognized me, she swooned, taking my hand and kissing it. I got out of my car and instinctively took this woman in my arms. At the same time, my dogs were running off with the other dog. I hugged her mistress as if she were a member of my family, my daughter, my sister. I felt a tremendous love fill me. When proximity is shared one-on-one, it really does a person good. It fills the heart. This is the kind of love that comes to us at a bend in the road, because it's her and because it's me, because of our animals; this is what I love, this is what I will hold onto as the "enchantment" of my life.

Finally, animals have saved me because they have offered me an old age that is beautiful and that I accept. I am serene and suffer from no frustrations. Before them, I had already done everything: been around the world, seen all of the famous people, the less famous people, places, situations, feelings. Yes, I've met a lot of people and I've seen a lot of things, and this is why I no longer want to see anyone. I've been around, and this tour has brought me back to animals. It has not sunk in that I am eighty-three. But, I lived my eight decades the way I needed to. My thirty-fourth year remains my favorite. At that time, I was the happiest, the most beautiful, and the most fulfilled. In my private life, I had come into everything that was best in me. This was also the age of maturity. I knew that I had squeezed out every ounce I could of folly, vitality, joy, recklessness, and browsing of all kinds. These were the years of assessment. I was very aware that what I had lived was wonderful and that going forward it could only be miserable. Up to that point, everything had been grand, gigantic, supersized: my successes, my joys, and my tragedies. I did not wish to experience worse and have only that to hold onto if everything had to come to an end. It was urgent that I change my point of view on existence, and from that point on, I started to imagine my life in a different way.

Like everything that is natural, I accept growing old. I believe we always lose what we have, and my youth, my beauty, and my freshness are no exception. There is not much left of my younger years apart from my soul, a child's soul that is still fascinated by many small things. I am amused and rendered hopeless by everything. I am also very naive, still easily taken for a ride. I am usually wary of things I needn't be, and I put my trust in things I shouldn't . . . I am very gullible and believe what people tell me.

I can't imagine being eighty-three years old, because I still see things with the same eyes. We don't grow older on the inside. Obviously, this does not exactly match the reflection I see in the mirror. I see the face of an old lady, of course, but also a lady who has lived. Each wrinkle sprinkled over my skin, each hollow, and each fold tells my story. Astonishingly, what I always loved most, my hair, has almost not changed at all. It has never been so long and falls down to my lower back. I am forced to pin it up in a chignon because I couldn't go about my life otherwise; it would get stuck on the back of my chair, the dogs would get their paws tangled up in it. I like my two-toned hair, the brown streaks of my natural color, the pieces discolored by yesterday's sun, and the superb strands of white that frame my face. Every day I do my chignon, and every day I put makeup on. I never see anyone, but I always take care of myself. And I always give myself a pedicure, of course—my feet are one of the most beautiful parts of my body. I also like my ears a lot: it's very rare to have such pretty ears! But I think I'm going to stop myself here.

And How Can Animals Save Us All?

Animals will save us when we change the way we look at them. When we decide to see them differently from how we do today: as ordinary resources, simple objects. I like to imagine a world where there is complementarity between our two species, a relationship of exchange and reciprocity. Humans would be more valiant if they were concerned about the well-being of animals. Opening their generosity to beings other than humans would be a historic step.

Respect. Now there's a great word for something natural.

We have believed for a long time that animals are like robots with paws. They move, run, eat, and reproduce by reflex. We thought it was impossible for them to think or imagine solutions if they found themselves faced with a problem. This is absurd. They are capable of thinking as well as inventing. We now know that bees came up with GPS before we did, that they use mathematics to calculate their movements and give information to other insects in their hive. Jane Goodall discovered that chimpanzees use tools to break the earth and remove termites in order to eat them. And before Dian Fossey agreed to have her photo published in *National Geographic*, holding a gorilla's hand, we thought this animal was an aggressive monster. One has only to look at the stereotypical images conveyed by the film *King Kong*.[1] Fossey showed us that this great ape was actually an herbivore, affectionate and peaceful.

Animal intelligence is unbelievable. But I regret that we must perform experiments—some that are grotesque—to prove this in order to respect animals the way they deserve. I've seen the experiments scientists perform: they put a monkey in a box with a drinking straw, or leave a piglet with several mothers to see if he can recognize his own. I don't like the idea that man needs to find a being intelligent in order to respect him. We compare ourselves in order to love. We measure the size of our brains, then we measure the capabilities of humans, big cats, marine mammals, primates, and horses to see how they measure up.

I embrace the animal mystery. I don't understand everything about their universe, and that's what I like. I observe an animal, he observes me, and a respectful distance between our two species is established.

---

1 *King Kong*, directed by Ernest B. Schoedsack and Merian C. Cooper, 1933.

Our differences form our synergies. Trying to manage everything in order to maintain control—out of fear of being surpassed by the unknown—is pathetic.

If We No Longer Used Animals, What Would We Do with Them? What Would We Become?

The great question . . . How many times have people asked me this? I am a vegetarian, not yet a vegan; I don't eat meat, but I still consume milk and eggs. This does not prevent me, however, from letting my animals live the way they want to. What I don't like is what goes against nature, mothers who have their little ones taken from them, endless births. Reproduction is a responsibility.

So, what will we do with animals if we stop killing them? Well, we will let them live, just as we let our own kind live! We will no longer allow factory farming, and we will recenter ourselves on what is most important; perhaps everyone will have their own cow. There won't be hundreds of thousands of them anymore, and the cow will become a rare but precious animal. I myself had a cow who brought me great pleasure. A living nativity had been set up in a shopping center near Saint-Tropez. A donkey and a heifer were watching over little Jesus. The cow was then supposed to be taken to a slaughterhouse. When I found out, I jumped in my Range Rover and threw some hay in it, left for Géant Casino, and brought the cow home with me! I named her Noëlle. She had the right to do whatever she wanted. She particularly enjoyed coming into the living room. Noëlle became so large that one day, she smashed the fence to go take a walk on the wild beach at La Garrigue. I then entrusted her to my foundation and the team at La Mare Auzou, where she was able to enjoy more space. She even had a little baby.

I am not nostalgic for rural France, nor do I agree with people who see old farms as the model for optimal animal living conditions. I do not have a very pleasant memory of my short experience on a farm. I got the impression that people simply did whatever they wanted to the farm animals. During the filming of *His Father's Portrait*,[2] right in the middle of the farm, the farmers were beating a pig with sticks, the geese were being mistreated, and dogs were tied up with a chain to a doghouse or an old barrel. Still, these conditions were better than the hell we are facing now. Today, life is no longer given its rhythm by the seasons: their existence is no longer respected for the survival they provide. It used to be the case that on farms, the annual pig slaughter was made into a ritual, it was a pause in time. We knew what the animal was offering us. I lived at a time when factory farming did not exist, when very few cows passed through the fields, and the ones who did were known by their farmer; they even had names. They were not just numbers or meat on hooves. Everything was still on a human scale: we lived, grew, and died with animals. Today, animals give their eggs, milk, and flesh in an assembly line.

We underestimate the benefits of being in contact with animals. Schools should be teaching their youngest students about respect for animals and the richness of the interdependent relationship we can have with them. Why not teach a class on animal-assisted therapy, a mediation between man and animal? Dogs, for example, can provide support for people living with social, psychological, or physical problems, and several experiments have shown that animals also are able to assist a person suffering from Alzheimer's disease. Animal-assisted therapy, or zootherapy, puts animals in touch with beings who are deprived of certain physiological capabilities but who also lack the spiritual

---

2 *His Father's Portrait*, directed by André Berthomieu, released in 1953.

perversions that frighten animals. As a result, the animals feel free, and this is why they are able to maximize their faculties. The contact between man and animal becomes one between equals. Animal to animal. I believe that my daily life is constant zootherapy. As an animal endowed with sensitivity and love, contact with dogs is crucial for me. Caressing them, touching them, and even smelling these animals brings me out of myself and elevates me as a human being.

An Animal Is Tamed by Trust

Animals are naturally afraid of humans. It is our self-seeking behavior that frightens them. So an animal is not tamed, because the idea of taming is already one of dominance, getting another creature to do what you want. Equality between beings helps lighten the load. When I first meet an animal who has been traumatized, for example, I can't greet him with my human dominance. When an animal has experienced shock, it becomes wild again, little by little. The bond I create with him should not be founded on trying to tame him, but on trust.

One of my dogs, Barbichue, has lived with me for five years. She was saved from a kill center. She was in such bad shape that she seemed irreparable: because of this, I let her do exactly what she wants. I don't require anything of her. She never comes to me and I don't go near her, either. It's a tacit agreement between us. She is aware only of my presence, and I think over time she will learn that she is not risking anything by being around me. I am allowing her to reestablish herself after her trauma in her own way. I don't try to intervene, because the last contact she had with a human being left her wounded and skittish. We found her in the dark, dying, surrounded by dead bodies. We know she endured countless tortures that left a profound mark on her. She is still wary and fickle, even with the other dogs, but she comes closer to me more and more often. She was given to me because it was believed that there was still a chance to regain her trust. Now, I never win over an animal's trust: he either gives it to me or he doesn't. He senses that I love him by instinct, and this is conveyed through only kind words or eye contact. It's a way of being. An offering.

The Opportunity to Offer Them A Second Chance

I maintain an unconditional love for all animals. I do not make a hierarchy between my companions. Each one occupies a very special place in my heart. I love my two little ewes, Frisette and Bigoudi, and my pigs, Cochonnet and Jambonneau—whose appearance amuses me quite a bit—but also my goats, my mare, and my little donkey. Over the years, my house in Saint-Tropez has become a refuge for animals who have been mistreated by life. My foundation, which protects and saves creatures every day, cannot treat every single tragic case. For more complicated situations, my team asks for my help because I have so many resources at my disposal: time, patience, love, and compassion. The animals who are given to me always have interesting stories. I welcome the sick, the broken, the old, the afraid, and the traumatized because nobody wants them, because they have been condemned to a miserable end of life. My donkey, Bonhomme, had been brutalized, showered with blows in the first years of his existence, and he continues to be wary of human beings, to such an extent that it is still sometimes difficult for me to approach him. We have known each other for ten years.

All of the animals who come and share my life have already been around the block a few times. I am always shocked to know that the creatures I take in have endured such mistreatment and torture. It's as if I myself experienced these horrible things. I couldn't possibly explain it, but I feel what they have been through, the evil they have been subjected to. Just as we observe in human beings, animal trauma exists and is very palpable. The suffering is still there; I can see it in their eyes. I offer these animals companionship and a new outlook. I try as much as possible to help them forget their past. I hope they forget, and that at some point they are unable to remember a single thing that was done to them. I don't know if I manage to calm them the way they need to be. It's not always possible. Some people from Annecy once gave me a little cat. She lived exclusively on the balcony of their apartment and always had an irrepressible desire to leave. She was also drawn by the void: she fell three floors down. Her bones were broken. Once she had healed, I adopted this fragile little creature. I offered her all the comfort she needed to rebuild herself, leaving the door open to meet her need for freedom, cuddling her, reassuring her . . . in vain. For four days, she stayed in a corner, not eating, not moving, hunched and completely unwilling to accept physical consolation. One day, I never saw her again. I don't know what happened to her. This truly pained me, because I had not been able to repair the suffering that she must have been reliving on a constant basis.

Taking on another person's pain and giving them love is also a way of giving myself energy; it makes me alive. I believe the world is hard and unjust by definition, and therefore compassion is essential. All human beings should be equipped with it.

Animals Are My Family

My human family exists but is far away. My close family is still made up of my animals. In *Initiales B.B.*, I tell this story: as a child, I used to make a racket with my sister, Mijanou. We were giggling uncontrollably until a Chinese vase fell and shattered. My mother's wrath was without end: she told us to address her with *vous*. I still remember her words: "From now on, you are no longer our daughters, you are strangers. Therefore, you will use *vous* when you speak to us." I was seven years old, and, all of a sudden, I no longer felt at home in my own house. I was in their house, my parents' house. After I married Vadim and my first earnings started coming in, I bought myself an apartment in Paris, La Madrague, and Bazoches. I wanted to feel at home and to never again feel excluded in the place I lived. In material terms, I had managed to put up with this suffering, but it was most definitely the emotional exclusion that was hardest to bear. If a child does not feel at home in her parents' house, she will not feel at home anywhere. She is in a permanent state of discomfort, instability, and insecurity. I felt like a stranger in my nuclear family because of this use of *vous*, because I could never be who I really was.

As a child, whenever I was around my parents, I often felt completely abandoned, alone, sad, and sometimes I even wanted to die. These are feelings that would keep coming back to me throughout my existence. Whenever I was in love with someone, I was always on a quest for a strong bond, a power, a life preserver to hold onto that would never leave me. Well, this is something impossible to find in a human being. I experienced many romantic disappointments with men who left me, and I suffered greatly. I am not someone who likes to be dependent on others, but I am dependent on love and attention; I am not at all a liberated woman in that sense. When someone left me, it was as if they had abandoned a dog. I was lost. Lost within my unquenchable thirst. And only animals could fill this immense void. No animal has ever abandoned me except by dying.

Mourning the Loss of an Animal

If there is one suffering that is unrecognized in this world, it is the loss of an animal. A life companion occupies such a place in a person's life that his or her disappearance creates a terrible emptiness. Why do we experience this atrocious sense of loss? Because animals lavish us with unconditional love, they give everything they have: their life, their love, their trust. We cannot recover from losing such a precious gift. An animal is a being with whom there is no conflict. We can argue with our family and be distant from our husband, our parents, or our friends. Not with animals. With them, the relationship is frank, clear, and continuous. I am always struck when I learn that a person has passed away just after their pet. The coincidence in these deaths says everything. In Scotland, someone told me about a dog who had lost his master. He had been at the burial, and when the coffin was put in the ground, the animal sat on the tomb and wouldn't move. Several times, the authorities tried to remove him, they tried closing the gates to the cemetery, but nothing could be done. He would always find a way to return to his master's grave. So, the people in the community gave up and came to feed him, and he never moved until his own death. The village buried the dog at the entrance to the cemetery, in the same ground as his master.

I recently received a letter from a lady who had lost her little dog following a surgical procedure. She had never woken up. Her letter was heartbreaking, and I decided to call her. On the other end of the line, I found a grief-stricken woman in total anguish. I think the worst thing about grieving the loss of an animal is that this sorrow is not understood and even ridiculed at times, which is even worse. Because animals play second fiddle in our society most of the time, harboring affection for them and mourning their death is not acceptable. Very often, other people do not understand our sadness. We are told: "You can't possibly be making a big deal about a dog," or, "It's just an animal, it's not as if a human died." All of these stupid phrases, from the point of the view of the person who's suffering, are only salt in a wound that unfortunately will never close.

The greatest challenge I have had to overcome in my life was the death of my setters. Lord, how I cried. The passing of Nini, the first in a long line, made me so miserable that I went to see a priest to get myself out of this dreadful pain. Alas, an animal can never be replaced. He is, and then he is no more. It is a love that is added to all the others, again and always. The feelings are renewed with each adoption. When one of my loves dies, the only thing that can soothe me is the affection of similar creatures, because they need me, just as the one before them had. I cannot deprive them of affection, of tenderness and attention, just because one of them has died. So, I am obligated to transfer the pain of the loss of this animal into the affection I have for the others. This can lessen the pain. A little. If I still feel a weight on my heart when I think of my little Nini, it's because we had an unusual bond. A golden thread had been woven between us. Nini was the dog who raced down to the edge of the yard at Bazoches, howling at the very moment my mother was dying. I was in Paris, holding Toty's hand. And the next morning when I called the caretaker at Bazoches to tell her about my mother's passing, she told me she already knew because of how my dog was behaving. Nini was extremely close to me spiritually. We shared a communion of our minds and souls. We looked at things the same way, as if we were connected.

I have never felt improper when grieving an animal. On the contrary, I have always felt that I carried something in me that was different from other people. I have never been ashamed to grieve for a dog, perhaps because I am always in mourning. Constantly dressed in black, I dress to mourn the loss of all my animals, and for all the animals who are forced to endure man's cruelty around the world. Animals who die—who suffer and die, because of men. I dress in mourning for animals in general. Black is not a color. It is the absence of color.

Who can judge me for this? To love a dog and to be loved by a dog is one of the most beautiful things I have experienced in my life. With whom could I have shared so much without being encumbered by words, phrasing, upbringing, or forethought? With whom could I have shared so many silences, apart from my dogs? It's a relationship that cannot be quantified, a relationship of caresses and glances and breaths. There is a world between us that takes years to construct. No one can understand the bond of love with a dog because it's a love that does not need words, a love that does not need proof, ceremonies, or get-togethers to exist. It is a love that recognizes the importance of the other being.

The Importance of Ritual

When you lose an animal, the ritual that follows—the burial—is very important. My animals' funerals are performed just like those we might offer humans: we come together, the people who knew him pay tribute, we make a hole in the earth, and I say a prayer. Then, each of us throws a fistful of earth to cover the little coffin. These small wooden cases are made by my caretaker or by a carpenter in Saint-Tropez. And every day I observe a time of silence in front of my small animal cemetery to think about all my friends. It's a very solemn place, located on a hillside. Among the little white crosses, there is even one that belongs to a young girl. I never met Bélinda, an adorable little girl who was stricken with a serious illness. We had kept up a long correspondence because she adored animals. They were her support, and she loved talking about them. When she died in 2004, she had articulated a last wish to her parents: she wanted some of her ashes to be scattered near my animals at La Madrague. I obviously agreed. Her parents came, and it was very emotional for all of us. We organized a religious ceremony with the priest of Saint-Tropez, and Bélinda's ashes were placed near my dogs. This young girl is right between them, just as she had asked. Her parents confided to me that our letter writing during Bélinda's illness had been a huge encouragement for her, and that she thought what I was doing for animals was miraculous. She wanted to be a part of this miracle, in her own way. I included her. She was twenty years old.

Places of rest are fundamentally important to me. I have immense respect for the dead and their last resting places.

Being forgotten after death is worse than death itself. I would rather die than forget my animals buried at Bazoches, La Madrague, and La Garrigue; they are my friends, my loves who sleep forever in Saint-Tropez and in all corners of France. I maintain all of my cemeteries, because it is our duty to those who have left us and no longer have the ability to take care of themselves. Naturally, I have already given instructions that the graves I take care of should continue to be maintained after my own passing.

Poof!

I am afraid of death. It terrifies me. The passing of my parents, close friends, and animals makes me think that death has been prowling around me forever and that I am constantly fighting against it. I have always done everything I could to prevent Papa, Maman, and my animals from dying. I would have done anything. But I always lost the battle. We can't fight it. There is a moment in life when the years have trickled away and those dear to you are leaving, one after another. Most of the men I loved have also passed.

When I learn about the death of the women and men who were my friends, my traveling companions, I don't cry; my emotion is intense but tucked carefully away. The passing of Jeanne Moreau, though, was a shock. I wasn't expecting it. The moment that filming for *Viva Maria!* was finished, we went our separate ways. We were opposites of each other. She had what I didn't, and vice versa. But the secret about movie careers is that they create special relationships between people. I spent three months with Jeanne on the other side of the world. We weren't friends, but an astonishing bond was forged between us from working in uncomfortable and sometimes hostile conditions. Jeanne was also a *Personne* with a capital *P*. She represented something, a new woman who had lovers and freedom. She highlighted a new lifestyle and way of expressing oneself. She lived as she pleased. This kind of personality is a positive influence on a society, and on those who rub shoulders with her.

When Mireille Darc left us—such a fragile and generous woman—I was deeply affected. I thought about her life, her battles, the love she diffused around her. After her passing, I spoke with Alain Delon, who was taking her death very hard. For the past few years, we have watched all of the people who populated our lives begin to leave us. But we are still here. Alain makes me smile, saying that we are the last two historical monuments of the twentieth century, the last cinematic representatives of a bygone era: our own.

So, those of us who remain—and there are not very many—come together like animals who sense that the end is coming quickly, like wild creatures who feel threatened. We all call one another. I was pleased to see Jean-Paul Belmondo when he came through Saint-Tropez, accompanied by the dog he had adopted from my foundation. I also share a rich friendship with Mylène Demongeot, who pays such special attention to animals. Astonishingly, I rarely see my old friend Robert Hossein, even though he is one of the most charming people I know. Like Alain, he is sensitive to the animal cause and has lent me his support in the past; these are the gestures that touch me and bring people closer together. When I think of Alain, I obviously think about the wild animal he is, the solitary animal. I cannot keep myself from finding similarities between us, and even more so today. I don't know why we never fell in love with each other. It's a good thing we didn't, though, because that would have been a catastrophe! He was too much of a star, and not the kind of man I wanted around me. I was looking for someone emotional, for kindness and tenderness. We also resembled each other too much. Alain is as a man what I am as a woman. This gives us something in common that is rather *uncommon*. We share the exceptional and the exception. If Alain ever makes the foolish decision to leave before I do, I'm going to be very angry with him. Losing him would be an inconsolable wound.

The idea of death paralyzes me. I am not sure that we find the people we knew somewhere else. What I would like best is for us all to disappear at once. Like in a film: "Poof!" We dissolve. An American series showed this scene: a man fell on a sidewalk, there was a puddle of water . . . and that was it. We die and there's nothing after. It's what comes after death, what happens to the body, that is really horrible. It's dirty. Cremation is not a solution because I'm afraid of burning and of fire. I'm unable to wrap my head around the idea of returning to the earth. I don't know if life after death exists. I don't know, and I don't necessarily hope for it. Who knows what craziness might still be waiting for us on the other side? We might as well sleep. Forever. We might as well rest. Maybe I'll finally be able to rest. I don't want to live to be one hundred, and I'd prefer not to know the date I'll be leaving. But I hope it happens quickly and without suffering. There's nothing worse than seeing those we love suffer.

My Inner Battles

I respect life unconditionally. Animal life, vegetable life, and mineral life. There is nothing more beautiful than life. When I think about the mystery of life, I can drown myself in questions. When something dies, man cannot breathe life back into it. It's over. Man can give death, but he cannot give life. There is something sacred and mysterious about life for me. I have watched the same strange occurrence so many times. A body is alive: it moves, it runs, it breathes, and then one day, it's no longer anything. It's nothing but hide, skin, a pile of flesh, a carcass. The small little something it had inside is no more. And what is that thing? We call it life; others give it a more spiritual meaning with the word *soul*.

The word *animal* comes from the Latin *anima*, which means breath, spirit, soul. *Animal* therefore possesses a Latin root carrying a spiritual dimension. I find this striking, especially because, for centuries, the animal was considered something without a soul, an old idea inherited from a Christian concept according to which offering animals a soul would overshadow the soul of humans.

Animals have a soul. And this certainty comes as the fruit of my experience. A soul is that mysterious part of us that makes us react to what is good and what is evil, to what should elevate us, or not, to what should enrich us or what should fill us with gloom. The soul goes beyond the body. I am not trying to develop a religious concept with this word, rather a concept of mystery. I respect the secret of life. It fascinates me.

Killing an animal, being responsible for cutting short its breath, therefore signifies that its life is not worth being lived. In the world today, animal life does not have importance or meaning. Our concept of life is centered on the human being. Our interests and our thoughts place man at the summit of creation, and the other species are forced to submit to the power over death that human beings have bestowed upon themselves. One wonders sometimes if the human species is really evolving.

Paule Drouault, a revolutionary animal protection journalist who is now deceased, used to say that we are not asking people to like animals, just to leave them the hell alone: I am absolutely in agreement with this opinion. Respect for life, for their life, is what is owed to every living being. In order to take advantage of his biological potential, an animal must be able to enjoy his health, the space he needs, the necessities of his kind, and his solitary or social nature. When the birth of a little panda took place at the Beauval Zoo, the news was welcomed with rejoicing. What hypocrisy . . . this animal was born in a cage, and he will remain there the rest of his life. The owners of lucrative game parks will tell us that what is most important is the survival of the panda species, which is what we are witnessing. Yes, the baby panda is in good health, but he is locked up. What he is being offered is the existence of a prisoner. With a life sentence. We put him in an incubator, we feed him with a bottle, we give him his meals at regular hours, and then we let him sleep under a plastic shrub—nothing too substantial—to make sure he's visible during the zoo's open hours. Wild animals are not animals who give birth in a clinic, they are not objects of entertainment. By managing the birth, life, and death of creatures when it suits our interests, we end up turning them into little robots.

And *if* birth in a zoo is such a curiosity, it is precisely because it is a rare event. Caged animals struggle to reproduce in captivity because their mental state does not allow them to benefit from their reproductive instincts. Who would want to give birth in these conditions? Who would want to have a baby to then leave him locked up in his room the rest of his life? Am I using what is called anthropomorphism?[3] No. I simply respect life.

In order to change things, to truly respect animal life, and to advance the cause, we would have to examine *who* we are. We would have to be capable of shame and pity. But these don't seem to exist anymore. Shame in the bullrings does not exist. Shame in the yards of a slaughterhouse does not exist. We are cruel to animals out of a desire for domination, out of indifference, cowardice, ignorance, sadism, and for our own profit.

---

3 Anthropomorphism is the act of attributing human behavioral or morphological characteristics to other entities such as animals.

What we do to animals shows what kind of humans we are. Our species, whose mental and technical faculties exceed those of others, should, in return, demonstrate respect, responsibility, and generosity.

Against a Disrespectful Humanity: Hippophagy

Eating horses: this is one of the things that proves to me the disrespect men have for animals. Horses and men have maintained one of the most noble relationships in history, and today the horse ends up on our plates. They are beautiful and powerful; they work hand in hand with men, and they are eaten in lasagna. This contradiction disgusts me.

I often compare horses and dogs. I cannot be indignant about the consumption of dogs in China and not revolt when France does the same thing to horses. Eating animals is horrible enough, but with horses I believe we are bordering on the atrocious. This animal has accompanied man so much throughout history: he was man's engine, his transportation, his farm tool, his weapon in battle, giving his life alongside man during countless wars. Horses are admired and ridden, and they bring in a great deal of money in horse races. To me, it would be a sign of gratitude—and the least we could do, really—to no longer eat them.

The heightened sensitivity I feel for horses goes back to the beginning of my battle. I met a former colonel, Roger Macchia, who had opened a shelter for horses called CHEM. As a participant in horse transports between Poland and France, and between the United States and France, he had witnessed horrific treatment inflicted on the creatures penned into enormous cattle cars. Roger had witnessed the suffering, agony, and terrifying deaths of animals transported in appalling conditions.

Naively, I didn't realize that people ate horses. It is true that I had already seen the heads of horses on the signs of horse butchers, but I thought it was for decoration. My parents had never given me horse to eat. Later, I learned that this custom had caught on during a very specific period of famine. During the Franco-Prussian War in 1870, when Paris was under siege, people pounced on everything they could for food: rats, dogs, zoo animals, and, of course, horses.

After meeting Roger, I wanted to see this with my own eyes. What I discovered that day in the year 2000 still haunts my nights. Those scenes are some of the most horrible I have ever had to look at. In Gorizia, on the border between Italy and Slovenia, I looked into the eyes of several horses sentenced to capital punishment. They were in transit, coming from Eastern European countries—in particular the Chernobyl region—to be taken into the European Community. They had even been examined with a Geiger counter. During their long days of travel, the horses had been crammed in against one another with nothing to eat or drink, shaken and trampled on. A mare had even given birth in one of the cars, and the little foal had been crushed by the other animals and soaked in their excrement, his eyes gouged out while his mother bled to death. Upon arrival, the doors to the trains, trucks, and cargo planes opened onto mutilated flesh that had to be removed with a crane and dragged to the slaughterhouse. The horses who were still standing upright, the ones who were aware of their fate, tried to escape. These creatures are extremely sensitive to abrupt movements and at that moment were in a state of absolute panic. They could sense death, and they tried again to escape it. The anguish in their eyes was nothing short of the ultimate animal despair.

I have always demanded that the French government abolish hippophagy. Four European countries still feast on horse meat: Belgium, the Netherlands, Italy, and, of course, France. Four countries that could all do without the consumption of this product.

I want to see hippophagy abolished before my death.

Against an Irresponsible Humanity:
The Abandonment of Dogs and Cats

It's not a big deal if a dog is abandoned. He or she is taken in by a shelter and will then be adopted by very kind people.

FALSE!

This is a fairy tale we tell children before bed so they can sleep soundly even though last night Papa and Maman left their dog on the side of the road. It never happens like that. Never. I'll tell you here about what really happens to the dogs and cats abandoned by their owners. I want to tell you why abandoning a pet is morally shameful and a despicable act of cowardice.

Shelters in France are spilling over with abandoned animals. Animals who have been tossed out of the car, who run after it to try and catch up until they're out of breath, thinking it's a game. Animals who are hung from a pole or a tree at night in the middle of the woods, condemned to a slow death. Or animals who are lucky enough to have an owner less cowardly than the others and are dropped off at a shelter and abandoned officially, with a certificate. In all of these cases, they are crammed in together, in all of these cases they live in crowded conditions, and in all of these cases they bark all day long hoping that their owner will hear them. In all of these cases, the dogs will wait for their owners, recognize them, and remain faithful to them if, by chance, they have a change of heart.

Alas, that never happens. And we end up euthanizing them.

It is urgent, therefore, to put an end to the mass reproduction of dogs and cats in France by sterilizing animals, outlawing sales in classified ads, prioritizing adoptions from shelters, and boycotting purchasing from pet shops and breeders to stop the trafficking of puppies from Eastern countries. Député Lionnel Luca, once an administrator in my foundation, had put together a private bill with this aim in 2005. Nothing came of it. People abandon their dogs as easily as they throw out a tissue. How can we do this? The foundation has done a lot of work on this increased awareness, what I would like to call the increased *responsibility* that each potential pet owner should take on. We have been working on this for years and have gotten nowhere. Is it too much to ask that people who want to adopt an animal do so with seriousness, scruples, love, faithfulness, and responsibility?

Let's stop behaving like children when it comes to animals. "I want this one today, but tomorrow I won't want it anymore." Certain battles are sometimes arduous, but eradicating dog and cat abandonment seems so simple to me. All it takes is loving the animal we share our lives with. We don't abandon those we truly love.

Against a Greedy Humanity: The Transport and Trafficking of Animals

In the first chapter, I discussed the massacre of innocent baby seals for the sale of their skin, fur, and oil. Unfortunately, one doesn't have to fly as far as that to see humans obsessed by their own profit. The transport of animals destined for slaughter in Europe is a black stain on the great humanist ideals that were born on this continent. Animals are considered merchandise.

In April 2017, with L214 and CIWF France (the latter is dedicated to the well-being of farm animals), we aired a video filmed in two slaughterhouses in Libya and Turkey. Cows born in France found themselves thousands of miles away, beaten, strung up while still alive, pinned to the ground, attached by rope tied around their hooves, their heads upside down, and their eyes poked out by the executioner's fingers before they were bled without any sort of desensitization. This torture is shared every year by nearly three million animals raised in the European Union and exported to Turkey, Eastern countries, North Africa, and the Middle East.

At the time, my foundation and the two other organizations I mentioned addressed an open letter to the French presidential candidates to encourage them to enforce a law that would limit animal transport to a duration of eight hours and cease all exports of living animals outside of the European Union. To no avail.

For over twenty years, we have actively protested against long animal transports: we have complained to the French minister of agriculture, of course, but also to Brussels. On September 21, 2017, we put forward a petition of one million signatures to the commissioner of Health and Food Security, Vytenis Andriukaitis. The regulations do not impose a limit on the duration of transports or on how densely they are packed, only on the layout of the trucks to promote ventilation and continuous control of the "cargo." It's torture!

My limited experience in the area of animal transport goes back to the year 2000 in Gorizia. With Ghyslaine, the director of my foundation, I went to see the tractor trailers transporting not only horses, but also seven hundred Hungarian sheep who had been locked up for over twenty-four hours, smothered in their winter wool by temperatures of 100 degrees in the shade, and able to stand only because they were crowded so close together. The sheep and lambs were bleating in misery. Finally, after a multitude of administrative formalities and procrastinations, we were able to get the poor little things into an aerated hangar. Little lambs two or three months old were knocking into one another to get out, releasing piercing cries, so similar to human newborns. Other little ones, already dying, were scattered across the floor. One of them, whose foot was broken, fainted. Despite our efforts to hydrate him, he died in my arms. I left with two lambs, saved from the hell that hundreds of others were being transported to. I am still bruised by this experience.

It's been seventeen years, and I know that things have not improved in any way. On the contrary. The animal condition is linked to the profit that can be exploited from them. The treatment we inflict upon animals today is the symbol of a society oriented toward materialism and consumption. Money is the nervous system of war.

In Vietnam and China, black bears are not exploited in shows, but on filthy "farms." Immobilized for life in minuscule cages, their abdomens are perforated by a tube implanted in their biliary duct. They are detained so that their bile can be collected and then sold at premium prices for use in traditional medicine and as a curative or aphrodisiac. These despicable farms were supposedly outlawed in 2006. But obviously, wherever there is profit, there is trafficking, and this ban has been blithely overlooked. The foundation has taken part in the financing of the Mekong Delta Bear Sanctuary and two other facilities—alongside Free the Bears and Wildlife at Risk—that have allowed dozens of bears to be saved. More recently, the Vietnamese Forest Administration (VNFOREST) and the NGO Animals Asia closed on an agreement to save these bears and to put a stop to this vile trade. I hope with all my heart that they will be able to bring this project to completion.

Soon, Africa will no longer be a land of elephants. Their natural habitats are being destroyed by the explosion of housing construction and farming activities, but this is nothing compared to the carnage caused by poaching. The international ivory trade has been illegal since 1989, but demand has been fed by the development of the Internet, clients without morals, and criminals. Each year, hundreds of elephants are killed for the illegal trafficking of ivory. In 1989, the first episode of the series *S.O.S. Animaux* I presented on TF1 was dedicated to elephants. The program encouraged an immediate commitment on France's part to suspend the importation of ivory. That same year, the African elephant was entered into the United Nations Convention on International Trade in

Endangered Species of Wild Fauna and Flora (CITES) Appendix I in the hopes of preventing its imminent extinction.

The fate of elephants continues to affect me. If elephants die, I die. I feel so close to them. Each time I learn about the killing of an elephant, I feel an intense grief in my heart. The elephant has always seemed like a kindred spirit to me: his spirit, finesse, and life philosophy guide me. I have learned a lot from observing these animals. The elephant is an extraordinary animal—EXTRAORDINARY—with an intelligence that makes man's pale in comparison. The organization of a group of elephants, for example, is based on a matriarchal society. Their language is made up of specific gestures and caresses. They are capable of "counting" the members of their group and solving complex problems. Their insight has been observed and proven many times. Elephants also have a little something that is somewhat unusual: they have an understanding of death. A sort of ritual is established when one of them dies. Often, when a mother is killed, the baby stays close to her for days and days. He waits. In vain. This is what led my foundation to take part in creating the first orphanage for elephant victims of poaching in Chad in 2001, under the guidance of Stéphanie Vergniault, a formidable and admirable elephant defender.

Elephants protect those they love. They are calm, and this serenity, this slowness in which they live, is equaled only by their wisdom. These animals are irreplaceable in the wild animal world. And it would seem that they are also irreplaceable as resources: this is why they are exploited for their ivory, used for transportation in Asia, and turned into pathetic attractions in western circuses and zoos. Bernard visits zoos regularly and was shocked by the sight of an elephant held in a confined space at one in southern France. There wasn't a tree or pool in sight. Elephants live in groups, and alone they waste away. All day long, this elephant turns to the left, then to the right, she turns to the right, then to the left, right, left, right, left . . . she was obviously going crazy. These animals are used to walking miles to find water and food. These are not creatures who are naturally sedentary and solitary; they live in groups, and they are even less suited to living in cages. Circus elephants are tortured to be able to perform like clowns, climbing on balls and playing the accordion with their trunks. All of this is grotesque, infuriating, and beneath them.

Why Are Animals Humans' Slaves?

Animals are the slaves and hostages of men.

The idea of freedom is indispensable to me. When I lived with my parents, I didn't have any. Until I was fifteen, I had a governess on my tail. I had been raised in a way that prevented me from expressing myself. I couldn't stand the rigidity, always having someone behind me, accompanying me everywhere. I couldn't take one step on the street without being chaperoned. I was constantly monitored, as were my friends, their backgrounds, and their parents. My parents decided everything for me: if I could spend time with this friend or that friend, if their parents were considered good people or not. It was insufferable. I had to break those barriers. When I married Vadim in 1952, the front door to freedom opened and never closed again. I was timid, so much so that when I was twenty-five, I went to the pharmacist on Avenue Paul-Doumer to ask him for a medication that could prevent me from blushing. As soon I said this, I blushed. The man told me that I needed to continue blushing because it was adorable. I think I have remained timid, but I was able to overcome my emotions and put myself in front of a camera or journalists when it was necessary, thanks to my own impertinence. It has been my weapon all my life. I developed this gift for repartee, sometimes even provocation, and often audacity, in order to free myself, to hide the shyness that was paralyzing me. All I had to do was be a little less timid, but instead I overshot. This is how I became what you've heard about.

Very quickly, I became aware that I didn't do things like other people. People say that I'm the symbol of women's liberation. In reality, I never thought I was carrying any kind of banner. At the time, I wasn't hoping for the liberation of women; I was only thinking of my own. This feeling of living in shackles, this lack of freedom on my own small scale has always stuck with me. And it is probably because I rejected it, because I wanted to break all of those chains, that I could never bear to see another vulnerable creature chained up.

I have always been horrified to see animals in captivity. The first thing that struck me and hurt me most was seeing birds in cages. At the beginning of my marriage to Vadim, we lived in a small and shabby building, and the concierge lived in a sad and cluttered room that stank. Only a small window overlooking a dismal courtyard, facing other buildings, offered the semblance of an opening. And in this universe was a small bird who used to sing inside a cage. This shocked me, and I asked this woman why she kept the bird in a cage. She responded, "Because he brings me a little life; I talk to him, he answers me." Why should we offer a living being an existence that is, in all respects, contrary to his nature? I have always refused to impose another nature on an animal or bend his instincts to suit my own pleasure or compensate for something I don't have.

Animals have always seemed fragile and vulnerable to me, defenseless, and I have always felt an innate need to protect them. Sometimes as a child, I had to spend time with my mother's friends and their "old lady dogs" who never ran and had to remain seated on their mistresses' petticoats. I thought to myself: "These poor little things, they're like toys." Of course they were fed, pampered, caressed, and allowed to sleep somewhere warm, but they were not considered to be individuals in their own right. They conformed to the rhythm of life that was imposed upon them. As a result, they were of course going against the needs of their kind. So to me, they were unhappy. Freedom is a fundamental right. Freedom is the right to be born, to live, and to die while respecting our species' primary conditioning, our nature. Freedom is the ability to be the master of one's human and nonhuman existence. No being, no living thing, should force another creature to bend on the pretext of that other creature's weakness.

When I decided to commit myself entirely to this animal battle in the early seventies, I was bothered by this idea of the exploitation of inferior beings. We were just beginning to question our relationship to animals. Until very recently, animals were usually regarded as resources or, worse, as machines. The idea of "animal liberation" was created by a British philosopher named Peter Singer. I had heard about the publication of his book in 1975 but unfortunately didn't read it at the time. In this work, he explains that animal liberation is a battle to defend the oppressed. This is most certainly my idea, as well. One hundred percent. When animals are held in slavery, they are seen as objects and not as living things. And just like slaves, their trade relies on profit. Like thousands of activists across the globe, I am hoping for the abolition of animal slavery today. To enslave one human being to another is abominable. At one time, we denied the pain and the humanity that the people in chains possessed. Today, we deny creatures their sensitivity and their "animality," in other words, their capacity to feel and experience things because they are alive.

This has become an urgent matter. Animals are going to disappear if there is not a rise in awareness and a rapid change. Many species we know today will soon disappear, the majority of which will be wild animals. A disconcerting phenomenon has also been observed: once they are hunted and pursued, when they no longer have enough numbers to reproduce, animals no longer have the will to do so. It is a sign of disturbing wisdom: they know by instinct that if they reproduce, they will be killed.

Where Are Animals Enslaved?

Where there is entertainment: circuses and zoos.

I was once part of a world that used animals. In all of my films, an animal was present. Alas, it was not always in the best way. In Vadim's film *The Night Heaven Fell* in 1958, I was playing the role of Ursula. In one scene, which was supposed to take place in Spain and had instead been filmed in a reconstructed studio in Paris, the heroine was supposed to be attacked by a bull in an arena. A young cow had been recruited for the occasion, and, to avoid danger, she had been given a sedative that was so strong she died before my very eyes. I had a very difficult time with this. I didn't know that this little cow had been drugged; she was standing in front of me, and I could tell something was wrong with her. She was drooling, and there was liquid coming out of her nose; she started breathing heavily and eventually lay down. I was so disgusted that I left and refused to redo the scene or continue filming. This animal was killed because of a film. For the needs of men. So they would be entertained. I carry this guilt inside me.

At the time, no laws existed about the use of animals in films. If an animal had to die, it was made to die. I am relieved that I never had to experience that kind of situation. I certainly could never have handled it. It wasn't until I ended my acting career that animals started gaining protection in the film industry. If it can really be considered protection.

The idea of animal-actors hardly pleases me. They are the equivalents of circus animals. Animal-actors are trained and shown in a way that is not natural. They are sequestered in a minuscule park and brought out to do their numbers. I don't like that; from the moment we force an animal to do something that does not correspond to his nature and his species, I am disgusted.

I once met an extraordinary dog in *The Novices*,[4] a movie I filmed with Annie Girardot. This German shepherd mix seemed to enjoy what he was doing. He would lie on his back and play, and he was always nuzzling us. In *Two Weeks in September*,[5] I had the pleasure of acting with a monkey. The experience of filming was splendid, thanks to him. He behaved like a baby with me, and I loved that. Monkeys and dogs are similar in this way: their biology and their areas of interest are both very close to man's. So their participation in films is similar to a game, an exchange. I believe that we must be careful to discern things based on the species we are dealing with. This is why all animal presence in a man's world must be controlled, justified, and, in some cases, forbidden.

We cannot say that science has made such and such discovery about a wild animal and then not take it into consideration. Circus trainers who attest to a privileged relationship with their wild animals make me uncomfortable, because the animals may not be thinking the same thing. We never ask them their opinion. We can love them and still be imposing upon them a certain promiscuity; we can love something and still deprive it of freedom. Above all, we must continue reminding ourselves of one thing: a wild animal is not programmed to jump up on his hind legs and roll over.

Circuses and zoos play on the illusion of happiness. Colors, magic, music, laughter, cotton candy, little nicknames for the animals, and voilà.

---

4 *The Novices*, directed by Claude Chabrol and Guy Casaril, 1970.
5 *Two Weeks in September*, directed by Serge Bourguignon, 1967.

It's very perverse. Everyone is drawn by the beauty of animals, and everybody wants to come closer to an animal from a faraway country. But how can we still be persuading the public that these attractions are not founded on constraint? What would it take to remind you that no animal willingly agrees to be locked up and trained? Training is never done without the use of force. One does not tame a wild animal, one subdues it. The constraints imposed on animals are exhausting and dangerous, because they put the animals in a state of disequilibrium. A trainer says that the dolphin is naturally playful, so he uses this as a justification for the game he will require the animal to participate in. It is true that dolphins, like sea lions, are more disposed to being tamed. But must we take advantage of their kindness and their sociability? Where is the line between play and constraint? In the world of zoos, animal parks, and the circus, where acts are performed, everything is based on the show and its profitability. So when the animal doesn't feel like playing, do we leave him alone? NO. We force him to play, therefore constraining him. So he is not free. And this is despicable.

We have been saving bears in Bulgaria since 2000. Bears used for dancing whose noses have been torn by the ring that holds them on a leash. These animals are dehydrated and skeletal when they arrive at the sanctuary we built in the countryside near Belitsa. The Dancing Bears Park is one of the largest bear reserves in Europe. There, they are able to enjoy a second life in their natural habitat, free, with no constraints.

When we cannot extricate animals from their degrading lives in show business, we try to protest on their behalf and raise awareness as much as possible. In 2005, the foundation organized a demonstration in front of the Parc Astérix dolphinarium to condemn the fact that the dolphins were being detained in conditions that did not meet their biological needs. We repeated this intervention in 2014 in front of the park basins.[6]

Some people have asked me to explain this paradox: orcas, tigers, and lions are wild animals, predators, and with one swipe of a paw they can kill a man: so why do they allow themselves to be subjugated? Here is my response: because of the animal vulnerability I spoke of earlier. Man uses the animal's weakness to subdue him and reduce him to slavery. And this happens via the traumatizing use of force. They may be beaten, starved, drugged, or forced to submit to horrifying living conditions. The animals in the entertainment industry know very well that if they do not agree to spin the ball on their nose, their treatment will become harsher. Why, then, do we still doubt animals' intelligence and their capacity for adaptation?

Whether an animal is enslaved in a circus or confined in a zoo, this is nothing short of oppression. It is everything I hate about humanity: domination and the unnatural. Why doesn't everyone else feel this same shock when confronted with animal slavery? Because they are attracted by the spectacle. This is the very definition of superficiality: seeing only the good side of things. What's behind all the decoration is always sordid.

I enjoy watching displays of human prowess and human performances at the circus, but I hate watching animals. They suffer from a lack of space and from stress from the noise of the crowd, interactions with visitors, and boredom. The battles my foundation has been leading for

6 Article from July 7, 2014, published in *Le Parisien*, "Des militants de la Fondation Bardot manifestent au Parc Astérix" (http://www. leparisien.fr/espace-premium/paris-75 /des-militants-de-la-fondation-bardot- manifestent-au-parc-asterix-07-07-2014-3982913 .php/). On July 6, 2014, ten Fondation activists interrupted the dolphin "show" at Parc Astérix. Description of the protest and photos can be found on the FBB website: http://www .fondationbrigittebardot.fr/s-informer/spectacles-d-animaux/asterix2014.

years are beginning to bear fruit, and French communities have started banning animal circuses from coming to their areas. In May 2006, we successfully liberated Natacha and Gandhi, two tigresses belonging to the Zavatta Circus.[7] We accompanied them to a nature park in Germany, the Lübeck Park, and from there they were transferred to a reserve in South Africa. The year after, we set in motion the rescue of a hippopotamus who was languishing in a truck with the Zavatta Circus. Tonga was transferred to a preserve in Sanwild, South Africa. It goes without saying that this environment was better able to meet his needs as a hippopotamus. The foundation even financed a large lake for Tonga. Afterward, we cofinanced the Tonga Welcome Facility in the Loire to welcome primates and felines seized from circuses or private homes.

Have you ever tried to look a zoo animal in the eye? Try it sometime. It's impossible. Their light has gone out. They are sad. So sad. Zoos are places where animals are humiliated and deprived of everything, even their desire to live.

I would much prefer that preservation take place in the area where the animals originate; I wish we could create enough reserves and national parks to prevent zoos from saying it was in an animal's best interest to live in a cage. Can we really accept the idea of locking an animal in a cell, even if we say it's for his protection? The mortality rate is elevated in captivity, and births are rare. Since it is now forbidden to capture wild animals, establishments simply make exchanges. They break up families. As soon as the animals are weaned, they are sent away. Animals in zoos do not live normally, and when a time comes when they are no

---

7 The rescue of the two tigresses was the subject of two long articles published in the foundation's *Info Journal* n° 57 and n° 62, in 2006.

longer needed, they are euthanized. Oh yes . . . animal slavery gives away their right to control both life and death.

I am obviously making a distinction between small zoos that resemble death houses and animal parks that are somewhat more like an animal's natural habitat. In parks, animals live in open spaces and they develop in semifreedom, with the priority being the conservation of the species. Incidentally, once you start taking care of animals a little in this world, you quickly realize that there is no longer anyplace on the planet that can really be called "wild" or "preserved" anymore. So, in the worst-case scenario, I choose the lesser of two evils. Animal parks can, to some extent, be a tool for preserving species because they are protected from poachers. We cannot imagine to what extent nature has become a confined space: the plains are covered with concrete, and the forests have been cut down. Even animals in the wild risk their lives every day. The great parks of Africa that stretch over thousands of acres are monitored in an almost military fashion by rangers. Did you know that poaching for elephant tusks and rhino horns takes place, most of the time, on the reserves? The rangers do not possess enough force to combat hunters armed with drones, machine guns, helicopters, infrared goggles, and armored vehicles. The poachers are soldiers at war to defend their black market.

Where There Is Torture: Fur and Animal Experimentation

FUR

What credibility do I have as a protector of animals if I have worn fur? This was the first argument from adversaries trying to turn my battle into an object of ridicule. And the answer I gave them has never changed: because I didn't know.

The horror of what was hiding behind a fur coat was unveiled to me little by little. In my time, it was spoken about very little, because few people could buy themselves this kind of item. It was not until I had my first earnings as an actress that I had the money to buy fur. One of the first things I bought was a mink stole to bring to the Cannes Film Festival. I never had anything to wear and was constantly agonizing about it, so Maman found me a coat at a reseller in Paris: a wrap that was so large I called it "my four-person mink" because it could have covered four people my size. Later, I also wore fur that had been lent to me by large boutiques to dazzle at one reception or another. It was soft, warm, sensual, and very enjoyable to wear. . . .

AND THEN I FOUND OUT. AND THEN I SAW.

This realization is one of the most significant in my life. I was so angry at myself for having strutted around with a skin of death on my back, a bloody hide torn off of a living being for my pleasure. This guilt mortified and damaged me. One day, I decided that this exterior sign of wealth was nothing more or less than wearing an animal mass grave on my shoulders.

Ever since, I have always wanted to fight harder and shout louder against this disgrace. I have answered questions in interviews and attended demonstrations like the one on November 19, 1994, that was heavily covered by the media. I really let them have it. My foundation launched a huge international call to collect furs, the symbol of this atrocious trade. And in front of the Paris Opera, Laetitia Scherrer, ex-model and daughter of a fashion designer,[8] burned clothing stained with blood. Soon after, though, the fashion industry took advantage of economic globalization, and fur was back in style in the runway collections and in winter accessories (collars, sleeve linings, etc.). In 1997, I responded to

8 Jean-Louis Scherrer, 1935–2013

Laetitia Scherrer's invitation to march in Paris on Avenue Montaigne, not far from the great emblems of French luxury. My friend Christian Zuber was present, as was the great humanist Théodore Monod. At ninety-five years of age, this magnificent man had lost none of his rage and was still fighting against the injustices done to animals. For this occasion, I wore an immense coat made with faux fur that Paco Rabanne had lent me. My objective was to show that it was possible to be elegant and ethical at the same time.

The fur industry involves the massacre of over thirty-five million animals every year who are bred and killed in horrific conditions. This is why my foundation and I are asking for the closing of French breeders. We called out this scandal when we learned that public funds had been allocated to the National Institute for Agricultural Research (INRA) to create the "Orylag," a breed of rabbit intended for, among other things, the production of fur. This poor animal is detained and butchered mainly in the Charente-Maritime region. As I mentioned in the first part of this book, the commercialization of dog, cat, and seal skin in the European Union is against the law. It is therefore humanely logical to forbid the sale of other morbid coats, whether they come from breeders or trappers.

It is so contradictory, and at the same time so outdated, that cruelty should be the symbol of luxury. Hundreds of fur farms are functioning today in the European Union. Mink, foxes, lynx, raccoons, and chinchillas are held as prisoners, exploited, deanimalized, and killed in conditions worthy of the grandest depictions of hell. Thousands of others are trapped, wounded, or left to die, like the coyotes whose fur decorates the collars of so many parkas. France has dozens of sites dedicated to breeding mink, poor little mammals man is only interested in for the financial manna he can take from them. The Émagny fur farm in the Doubs region is the site of regular demonstrations,[9] and its numbers are expected to double, which outrages me.[10]

The martyrs of the fashion world are piled into minuscule cages where they live with their peers in their own excrement, often developing abnormal behaviors like self-mutilation, hoping to get themselves out of the abyss. The animals are sacrificed at the age of six or seven months, after the molting that masks all of the flaws in the fur. Then comes the moment of death. I am writing these lines as a plea, because describing this horror makes me tremble. Animals intended for the production of fur—a material that will be sewn, sold, and displayed in runway shows, photos, and videos around the world to be admired by people—are the victims of hangings, broken necks, gassing, injections, poisonings, and electrocutions by the mouth or anus. . . . My God! The worst part is that these methods are as ineffective as they are barbaric. At the foundation, we have collected testimonies that would make a person shudder: many animals "wake up" during the dismemberment!

What I wish for, obviously, is the plain and simple end to the use of animal fur. I can do nothing but applaud the initiative of brands like Gucci who are leading by example and refusing from now on to place an animal graveyard on their models' bodies. But I am still speaking out vehemently against fur farming in France, even though Switzerland, Austria, Great Britain, and Hungary have already outlawed it. Do we not understand that synthetic fur is comparable to animal fur? Even Karl Lagerfeld has recognized this.

---

9 The list and description of various movements against the Émagny fur farm since 2012 can be found on the foundation's website: http://www.fondationbrigittebardot.fr/agir/participer -a-une-manifestation/ fourrure-non-aux-elevages-de-visons.
10 Article on the website of France 3 Bourgogne-Franche-Comté from July 21, 2017, "L'élevage de visons d'Émagny autorisé à s'agrandir," http://france3-regions.francetvinfo .fr/bourgogne-franche-comte/doubs/ elevage-visons-emagny-autorise-s-agrandir-1300865 .html.

Animal Experimentation

What tribute must the animal owe to man that he must endure such suffering? Is the animal so indebted to human beings that he must pay with his life? I'm not going to beat around the bush here: animal experimentation is not a necessary evil—it is evil. Period. These methods are immoral. First of all, why would it be unthinkable to perform these tests on men, women, and children? Because they are human, living beings, and sensitive to pain? Or because torture is not ethical? So why does morality evaporate when animals are involved? Because they don't have the intelligence and reason that humans do? That is the wrong answer.

The rabbit feels the same pain we do when inflammatory products are injected into his eyes with a needle. It's what is known as the Draize test. The white rabbit is placed in a restraint where only his head is visible. Chemical substances are introduced into his eye sockets again and again until the eye is totally destroyed. Animals experience the same misery as men when they are put in contact with agricultural pollutants, pesticides, and other products, and when they are tested for photosensitivity under an ultraviolet lamp with their hair shaved to determine at what moment the skin starts to burn. And finally, a monkey suffers the same psychological disturbances a small child does when he is isolated at birth, continuing for months and years with no contact, in the context of a very common experiment called "affective isolation" or "maternal deprivation."

Animal experimentation is horrible because it is a slow death perpetrated in a medical world whose primary aim is to relieve suffering. Because scientists can still be torturers. Throughout my battle, I have witnessed scenes of horror that still turn my blood cold today. I remember a photo of a herding dog who had had the head of a Pomeranian transplanted onto his neck. There was also an ape whose body was split open with tubes, disemboweled but still conscious, the electrocuted monkey, and a cat whose skull had been drilled through with holes. For an episode of *S.O.S.* dedicated to animal experimentation in 1989, we had broadcast a video of a sow screaming and thrashing under jets of napalm, the same kind used in incendiary bombs. Transformed into a living torch, this poor pig took several long minutes to die, burnt to ashes. I will never forget the looks in those thousands of animals' eyes: full of anxiety, unhappiness, pleading. Deep eyes that accept as much as they refuse and reflect this abnegation and outrage, this hopelessness mixed with infinite sadness. The guinea pig's white eye, begging for the end of an ordeal that goes on forever.

Animal experimentation is indecent because it is a cruelty that is often disputed. Protectors of animal rights get bad press when they criticize vivisection. We are considered to be "antiscience," unworthy whiners who are trying to soil the tests that are performed "for our own good." However, these very admirable words like "test," "experiment," and "scientific" hide a terrifying reality in which millions of laboratory animals are butchered every year, the majority of the time without anesthesia due to a lack of time, resources, or sensitivity. Added to this are the animals' prison-like detention conditions. They only come out of their cells to be "worked on," pushed, and collared with the help of rods and clubs. Most of the time, the animals thrash about and cry, so they are subdued by force, and, in the most extreme cases, their vocal cords are cut.

Animal experimentation is shameful because it is obscure. People don't really know where it happens. This goes for the large pharmaceutical laboratories, of course, but also the universities, the veterinary schools, the military research centers, and the public institutes of toxicology and agronomy. Unfortunately, these great testers don't share the results of their research with one another the way they do with experiments performed on humans. There are also experiments performed purely for scholarly purposes so that researchers can write and distribute journal articles.[11] The Animal Testing Association needs to lift the veil on the trials performed at the Maisons-Alfort veterinary school. Dogs being held in extreme suffering are condemned to a long life of agony.[12] Painful experiments are performed without anesthesia because certain protocols specify that the use of analgesics might "interfere with the results." Another investigation revealed that more than 850,000 mice are sacrificed each year in France.

Finally, animal experimentation is perverse because it is backward. We are sacrificing living beings, and, at the same time, we are able to visit the moon and create atomic bombs, robots, and computers. Our humanity is becoming virtual: except for our crimes. For is there a line between science and sadism when the majority of experiments on animals are performed while they are still living, when their cries are muffled, when these creatures are curling up in their cages to escape their torturers? Where is the respect for life when the guinea pigs who are used are thrown away like ordinary latex gloves as soon as they have died for us?

There are a great number of "guinea pigs" who are forced into this life of slavery: rodents, birds, pigs, rabbits, cats, primates, horses, and dogs— beagles in particular. These tricolored little dogs are appreciated for their sweet nature and their great loyalty. Today, only research on great apes like orangutans, bonobos, gorillas, and chimpanzees is forbidden in most countries. The fact that they are so biologically close to humans makes us slightly uncomfortable at the thought of seeing them in a lab.

---

11 Thank you to journalist Guillaume Pot, who is part of my battle against vivisection.
12 The partial investigation was revealed in December 2016 by Animal Testing and PETA (https://animaltesting.fr/2016/12/01/une-vie-de-souffrances- les-experiences-sur-les -chiens-financees-par-le-telethon). An article on the subject had been published in 2013: https://tempsreel.nouvelobs.com/rue89/rue89-nos-vies-connectees/20131203.RUE0629 /experimentation-animale- les-chiens-cobayes-face-cachee-du-telethon.html.

Laboratory guinea pigs are created for this purpose and come from breeders to meet this demand. These animals are sometimes the victims of sordid trafficking, like the famous network of stolen dogs in Lot-et-Garonne. This minor news item caused an uproar in the late eighties, and I attended the hearings with my friends Dany Saval and Nino Ferrer. We have protested regularly against the establishment of breeding facilities for animals who will be sold to laboratories. In 1999, I went to the Allier region to prevent the opening of a farm for two thousand dogs. As it happens, we were supported by the majority of the French people: according to an IFOP survey, 87 percent of those surveyed were against the opening of new breeders for dogs who would be used in laboratories.[13] In 2005, my foundation was able to free thirty beagles who were being escorted to Croatia for experimental purposes. A national mobilization allowed these dogs to be recovered and adopted. Animals also come from outside the country. As a side note, you may be interested to learn that the jewel of our national economy, Air France–KLM, remains the last large airline company that still transports primates used in scientific trials,[14] despite our many letters asking them to stop this trafficking.[15]

As you may have guessed, animals very rarely escape this life of torture. The majority are sacrificed, euthanized, incinerated, or thrown in the trash. The others, the lucky ones who still have a few useable limbs,

---

13 Source: Fondation Brigitte Bardot
14 "Primatologist Jane Goodall attacks Air France over its transport of primates," *Le Figaro*, May 26, 2014 (http://www.lefigaro.fr/actualite- france/2014/05/26/01016-20140526 ARTFIG00223-le-primatologue-jane- goodall-attaque-air-france-sur-le-transport-des -primates.php); "Demonstration calls for Air France to stop primate transport," *Le Parisien*, August 30, 2017. (http://www.leparisien.fr/societe/defense-animale-happening-pour-qu -air-france-arrete-le-transport-des-singes-30-08-2017-7223700.php).
15 Letter from Brigitte Bardot to the P-DG of Air France on December 30, 2016, can be found on the foundation website http://www.fondationbrigittebardot.fr/experimentation -animale/actualites/airfrance.

Brigitte Bardot at the London Zoo, 1966.
Courtesy of Marc de Raemy

BB's iconic shot during the 1977 campaign to end the hunting of baby seals.
Courtesy of Marc de Raemy

BB on her estate in Bazoches (continued opposite page).
Courtesy of Marc de Raemy

BB in the fields of Bazoches.
Courtesy of Marc de Raemy

BB in her apartment on Boulevard Lannes in Paris.
Courtesy of Marc de Raemy

Brigitte Bardot.
Courtesy of Marc de Raemy

BB with a dog and bird.
Courtesy of Marc de Raemy

Watson the donkey (top) and Auzou the horse (bottom) receiving BB's affection.
Courtesy of Fondation Brigitte Bardot

Brigitte with cows (above) and fawns (below).
Courtesy of Fondation Brigitte Bardot

BB at Gévaudan Wolf Park in Saint-Léger-de-Peyre, France.
Courtesy of Fondation Brigitte Bardot

may be offered up for adoption via the wonderful organization GRAAL. But they are a minority.

I myself took in a survivor of this hell. In 1980, for an episode of the television show *Les Dossiers de l'écran* on Antenne 2, I participated in a roundtable discussion on animal experimentation. This took place after the release of a film by Allain Bougrain-Dubourg showing the vivisection of a dog at a hospital in Choisy, which is almost unbearable to watch. In it, a small boxer is being tortured: her heart, her lungs, and her entire respiratory system had been removed and were to be replaced with a machine. The little dog was heavily sedated. She was supposed to die at the end of the experiment. I was outraged and demanded that she be revived. She didn't come out of her coma for two days. Afterward, I picked up her body, though it could no longer really be called one; it was more like a scrap of flesh with all of its parts sewn back together. She had paid so dearly for this surgery that she deserved a more than sublime survival. I took her with me. She was moaning, no longer having the strength to cry out. She was always cold. Allain and I covered her, cared for her, and stood by her while she learned to walk again. We taught her to feed herself. One scar remained, though, and it was psychological. The little boxer was terribly weak and fearful. As soon as she saw a man, she would hide under a piece of furniture. I named her Amélie, in reference to the play *Occupe-toi d'Amélie* by Georges Feydeau. Amélie ended her days happy at La Garrigue. Sometime after her operation, I learned that the machine that was supposed to serve as her respiratory substitute had been used during an operation on a little girl. Amélie had saved this child's life. Yes, science can save people; this is a certainty and I am very happy about that, but this story with Amélie goes back to the early eighties, and I find it hard to believe that today, so many years later, we can't make more of an effort to implement alternative solutions, substitutions, or replacements that could undoubtedly avoid animal suffering.

The fight against vivisection is one of our great battles at the founda-tion because we believe that the use of the animal model is outdated. In 1992, we lobbied the European Parliament to ban cosmetic testing. The European Union finally opted for a total ban in 2013. Today, we hope to continue this battle in the medical area because, besides being immoral, animal testing is also scientifically questionable. The scientific commit-tee that serves as a reference in this area, Pro Anima, has already explained that tests on animals do not necessarily suggest that the results will be the same in humans. Because each species is different, the reac-tions vary from one body to another. This makes one wonder about how reliable these methods are. In a way, animal experimentation might actually be interfering with test results, therefore posing a threat to humans.

The animal model has reached its limits. Before a medication can be commercialized, it must undergo clinical tests on animals, but it's incor-rect to assume that this is the most surefire method. Everyone knows this, but no one wants to do what it takes to adopt other methods. And yet they exist. In vitro techniques that use human cells and tissues, and in silico techniques that are based on computer-generated models, are both replacement methods that have already proven to be effective. Three-dimensional technology allows diseases to be turned into models and miniature organs to be constructed. But the budgets offered to sci-ence don't include research on alternative methods. So, beginning in 2008, my foundation cofinanced "Valitox," a testing program supported by Pro Anima. The objective is to find alternative testing methods, par-ticularly for the acute toxicity of chemical products. But as of 2018, this test has still not been approved by the European Union Reference Laboratory for Alternatives to Animal Testing (ECVAM). This has been dragging on for ten years in spite of the numerous tests that were required and passed with success.

The European Union now has the ethical obligation to revisit its position on research. Politicians, too, must work to finance a science that is effective and more humane in order to fight against opacity, ideally with testing centers controlled by an independent and transparent authority. We are dealing with living beings, and everything that involves the manipulation of life should be public knowledge.

I am sick to my stomach as I write these lines. I don't want to live in a society that tolerates animal experimentation. If science is insensitive, if science doesn't have a conscience, then who will have one? Certainly not the large pharmaceutical firms that are at the root of all of these horrors and are also fearsomely powerful.

Where They Become Nothing: Intensive Animal Farming

When I started criticizing the way animals were being killed in 1962, I never imagined that fifty-five years later I would be condemning the way we force them to live. "Live" is a rather strong word, though. In truth, they survive; they are kept alive, which is unfortunate for them because death is a lighter sentence than a life in intensive animal farming, or factory farming. It is Dante's Inferno; a hellish cycle, a sentence to life imprisonment. All this for a crime that these animals have not committed. Animals in this context are no longer living creatures, because they are deanimalized. They are objects, things, machines that must produce in record time. Nothing about this is natural.

The majority of affordable or lower-quality meat today comes from animals who are locked up for their entire lives in buildings that are filled to bursting. Everything is oriented toward production, always more and always faster. Enormous quantities of meat, milk, eggs, and animals come out of these factory farms. The animals are confined without air, without light, and without rest.

Farming is considered "intensive" when:

- Only the best animals are kept, selected based on their sex, and then confined in enclosed spaces.
- The small size of the space where animals are concentrated prevents movement, and basic care (hay, ground to explore) is not provided.
- Animal growth is accelerated with the help of medication, antibiotics, or force-feeding methods, and the females are continuously inseminated.

The inexpensive ham you buy may come from sows who lay constantly on one side in their holding cages while their piglets suckled their necrotized teats for just a few days before they were separated.

Maybe your pork chop, bought vacuum-packed, comes from an animal who was castrated without painkillers (a necessary procedure on a factory farm), who had his tail cut off without painkillers, and who had his teeth filed. Without painkillers, of course.

Your little Sunday veal, served roasted, may have had his horns amputated, obviously without anesthesia. He may also have had respiratory problems and digestive issues and probably "lived" next to a few dead calves because 10 percent of the little ones cannot survive in such conditions. This calf may have been weaned in a day. One day. Are you aware of that? You're eating a baby.

I'm not finished yet.

Certain milks you offer to your children may come from cows suffering from mastitis, an inflammation of the udders that affects all animals who are not given any respite. The sensitivity of the udders makes milking extremely painful for the cow, and the inflammation leads to a flow of pus that ends up in the milk that is consumed.

The lamb for your gigot may have never been able to move because of his pneumonia or joint problems; he never had time to learn to walk and was held in a space so small he couldn't sit down.

The chicken *suprême* served in the restaurant may have had feet that could no longer support his weight, because as a baby chick he was forced to finish growing in three weeks.

The duck you're dipping in sweet and sour sauce may have suffered from liver issues, heart trouble, and diarrhea. Why? Because waterfowl are perpetually force-fed.

Maybe the egg in your *œuf à la coque* doesn't have the vibrant and shiny orange of the egg that comes from a hen who runs around in the open air on green grass. Maybe it has that strange, drab, industrial yellow of hens who are kept immobile their whole lives, their bones in tiny pieces.

As a starting point for hopefully putting an end to these other abuses, in 1996, I requested and obtained a ban on horse caudectomies from the minister of agriculture. This painful mutilation consisted of severing the caudal vertebrae and cutting the tail, all for aesthetic purposes, out of snobbery and stupidity.

But the battle is long and very difficult, because factory farming is a corrupt system. It is an inhumane form of capitalism. The animals are machines: piled together, pushed to produce, then slaughtered. The animals are slave laborers without rights. They are unable to walk properly, much less run or fly. They are forbidden from spending time with one another or reproducing naturally, because they are artificially inseminated. They don't even have the right to their physical integrity: their tails and beaks are cut, as I've said, but so are their wings, their claws, their testicles, and their teeth.

Farm animals are considered sentient beings in the eyes of the law. But not when it concerns their lack of oxygen and natural light, or their distress when they are ripped away from their mothers. The notion of life in these farms is nonexistent. Nobody cares. These are flesh and meat factories, not wellness centers.

Factory farming is a violation of the dignity of the living being that every animal is, and it is a shameful act perpetrated by the being that man has become.

Who Are the Enemies of Animals?

MAN: DOMINANT AND PREDATOR

I have never asked myself the question of whether one species is superior or inferior to another, even though I will admit that some are more gifted than others. Within the animal world, man has been able to develop his intelligence to modify his environment. And when an individual is evolved, he has an obligation to care for defenseless and voiceless beings. Since we have an advantage, we should be using to it to protect them, not to torture them.

"Speciesism"

Today, we often hear people talking about "speciesism," the practice of attributing greater importance to one species over another. To me, this is animal racism. Man is not superior to animals. This is a physical, natural, and emotional fact. Man has unequaled intellectual faculties, but these do not give him the right to dominance over other living species. *There* is the injustice. *There* is the mistake. I find the word "speciesist" complicated, but it does a good job of defining this idea because it brings to mind a kind of "ranking" of creatures.

What I find horribly shocking is the way that governments and hunters label certain animals as "pests." If an animal eats what the hunter is hunting, he is called a pest. Hunters tell us these animals cause damage to agricultural activities and to other flora and fauna. In reality, they reproach the "pests" for being predators just like them, and for going after pheasants, hares, and other game. Foxes, magpies, crows, coypu, and wild boars, on the other hand, are called pests simply because they bother humans—that's the only reason! So, humans are allowed to kill them all year long, outside the hunting seasons, anywhere, anytime, and in any manner. Methods range from simple shooting to trapping and dragging them out of their dens. During fox hunts, dogs are cruelly sent down into the fox's hole, and when the animal comes out, panicked, the hunter kills him at point-blank range!

Grouping animals into categories is speciesism. It not only presumes that the human being is superior to the animal being, but also, and more significantly, it establishes a hierarchy between animals that is based on our needs. A dog is more important than a cow, a lion is viewed more positively than a pig, and a rat is less respected than a dolphin. One animal is placed in the domestic box, another in the butcher's, leisure, wild. . . . To me, they are all equally worthy, they are all the same. We are only one species among millions of others on earth, but for some reason, we have decreed that only our race can decide for the others.

All of the animals around me have their own place. I caress my pig the same way I caress my chicken, my cat, or my dog. When we live our daily life in symbiosis with our animals, the interactions we have with them are often incredible. I used to have chickens at Bazoches, and every day, one of them would climb up the small staircase that led to my bedroom to lay an irreproachably clean egg on my pillow. One might think that a chicken has no business being in a bed, or that a pig shouldn't be in a kitchen, so what on earth would people think about the goat who slept in my hotel room with me while I was filming a movie? Even though I usually sleep with my dog and not my pig, it is not because the former is superior to the latter; it's just that my dog is more used to my bed than my pig is! All species share the same qualities: they can feel a gentle touch and pain, they need freedom, and they need others. Even the most solitary among them.

Might Makes Right

When we find ourselves in a position above others, the worst thing about this is the right that we give ourselves over them. And today, man has given himself every right. He does not simply feed himself, he wastes; he does not simply get dressed, he pillages; he does not simply amuse himself, he perverts. The additional powers of reason that humans possess in comparison to animals should force us to go beyond our predatory nature, because the two sides of this battle are not equally armed. Our power today is not physiological: if a man fights a bear with only his bare hands, I would bet that he's not going to win! Our power today lies in our mental faculties and our technical intelligence that enable us to adapt ourselves to all circumstances. There are no more limits, there is no more moderation.

"Man is at the center of the Earth, he is the master of the world; nature, therefore, is his resource." I find this whole idea intolerable. The documentary *Home* does an excellent job of showing man's possessive frenzy,[16] as well as the progressive destruction of the Earth, the theft and violation of all its riches, its surfaces, and its undergrounds. Possession is a terrible human trait; we always want a little more of something; as a result, the earth has become Swiss cheese. This frenzy is idiotic. The planet can no longer absorb all of the human beings who are wrecking everything. The women and men who destroy flora are the same as

---

16 *Home*, documentary written and directed by Yann Arthus-Bertrand, 2009.

those who destroy the fauna. Is man more evolved and better evolved than the others? Yes. He has a genius capacity for construction. But also for destruction. We all have a common history. We are descendants of the same Everything, the same tree. And I endorse this golden rule: there should be a balance between nature, animal, and man. And if this equilibrium is broken, the world's ecological chain will no longer function. And man will be the first victim.

Religion

Religion is far from tender toward animals. Their damaged and degrading image in our cultures comes in part from religious texts and dogmas.

I have never felt comfortable with the idea of religion. I prefer a free spirituality, a direct relationship with Heaven. I have read very little of the Bible; all of those texts bore me. I like the Holy Places because they are beautiful. As I said, it's the spirit that moves me, wherever it leads. The rest—the laws, the advice, the denominations—I don't care two hoots about. But I understand that certain people, hopeless or not, need to believe.

The idea of transcendence is present in the personal relationship I have with the Virgin Mary. This faith is so well nurtured that she and I have a very close bond. It happened little by little. Now I go to meet her whenever I feel like it, the way I would with a dear friend or a mother. I speak to her frankly, no blah-blah, and sometimes I don't say anything at all; I speak to her with my heart. I tell her when things aren't going well, I give her the details of my problems, I tell her this and that. I confide in her about my pains, my joys, my hopes, and my passions. I communicate with her as I would in a real-life conversation, not just in the context of a request or a plea. A long time ago, I had a small chapel built at La

Garrigue. I only go there now on rare occasions. It is perched on a hill surrounded by thyme, pine trees, rockroses, and terebinth trees. The footpath is rocky, and taking it on my crutches these days is a true pilgrimage. But I like to go there because I can speak openly with the Blessed Virgin. One day, I was up there with my dogs, and Bernard heard me shouting. I was furious. "Who are you so angry with?" he asked, and I answered, "My little Virgin Mary." She had not helped me as she should have in a difficult moment.

The Virgin Mary has stood by me for a long time. Her presence is intimate and benevolent. I am supported by the idea of gentleness, purity, and light that she inspires, her sense of unconditional generosity and maternal protection. She, too, suffered while she was on Earth.

The greatest pain she experienced was the loss and the crucifixion of her son; I am so touched by this truth. She has experienced pain in her body and soul, and so she cannot help but be sensitive to the pain of others. When I lose an animal and am deeply sad, I ask Mary to help me. She protects me, I know she does. I know she has been there for everything I've been through, from the life's extravagances to death's attempts to take me. Yes, she answers my calls, and I believe this because I would not have been able to overcome challenges that came my way if I had not been helped. If she had not accompanied me with her mercy at the appropriate moment, I would have been dead a long time ago. I'm convinced.

I had a religious upbringing, and I made my First Communion, went to catechism class, and visited the nuns. My parents were believers and practicing Catholics. But I hold the idea of religion and its hierarchy at a distance. The "ministers of God" I met were often disappointing, apart from rare exceptions, like Father Pestre, one of my great friends and founder of the Saint-Roch refuge in Marseille, who organized demonstrations against the barbaric things done to animals and donated the collection from his masses to help them. I am also in contact with a religious man in Alsace who maintains a small chapel with almost nothing and built a garden next to it where animals can be buried.

Religion always makes me think of immobility. Its structures do not change, and the people in those structures seem static. They have done nothing to help us love animals, plants, and nature. Instead, they push us to establish ourselves as dominators. In the Bible, man reigns without compromise over plants and animals, and at no moment are they given a soul. Only man carries this asset, because according to the Scriptures, he has been made in the image of God: he is therefore above everything. The right to govern all of creation, to use and abuse other species, stems from this divine superiority. Animals are not yet machines in the Bible, but almost. Their existence depends on their cooperation with man, and their death is a means to domination or purification. Consider the idea of sacrifice, for example. Animals have always been used to worship the Lord, and Abraham himself used a ram as a substitute for his son, Isaac, whom God had just spared. Incidentally, I have always wondered who this God was that everyone said was good, but who also allowed an innocent animal to be killed. Because the herd was the greatest source of wealth a family could have, offering a ram to the Lord was considered a sign of devotion, and by doing this, men were cleansed of their sins. The same is true of the scapegoat who, in the Old Testament, was symbolically burdened with human sins before being sent into the desert.

Unfortunately, we have not abandoned the idea of animal sacrifice. The lamb is still killed for Easter, just as the sheep is during Eid-al-Kebir. For ages, we have believed that the spilled blood of an innocent victim gives value to a celebration, a ritual, or a pardon. Why do people not opt for another tradition on these occasions? Because it is a habit, a bad habit. And also because, today, the blood is spilled far away from us in the horror of the slaughterhouses, and because the sacrificed creature no longer resembles a lamb skewered over a wood fire, but instead a tidy leg of lamb that we put in the oven with little vegetables. Without knowing it, every person who tastes the Easter lamb is party to the idea of sacrificing the Lamb of God. "Lamb of God who removes the sins of the world," the song says, but if every family today had to kill their own animal in order to eat it, I can assure you that the number of vegetarians would explode. Which reminds me of this story: One day, Tolstoy was sitting down to a meal with his family when his elderly aunt found a live chicken and a knife at her place at the table. This woman had notified the author, who was a vegetarian, that she wished to eat meat at the meal, and Tolstoy explained that if she wanted to eat chicken, all she had to do was kill the creature herself!

Taking care of animals requires true spiritual charity, no less than is required to care for the weakest humans. And if I feel so distant from the idea of religion, it is because it carries in it great violence: its rules and restrictions are drastic. Freedom does not exist in religion; the organization of each denomination is so sectarian, people are pitted against one another and defend their own corner, each one believing they hold the Truth. Not to mention that the texts are contradictory. In the case of animals, for example, certain writings encourage sacrifice without mercy, while others reject the animal martyr.

The religion, or rather the philosophy, that is most respectful of animals is still Hinduism. As a vegetarian, Gandhi always insisted that eating meat gave a person the taste for blood. I see it the same way: eating meat turns you into a carnivore. We need only observe the divergence in behavior between carnivores and herbivores in the animal world. Deer, sheep, and elephants are some of the least aggressive species, unlike lions, sharks, and crocodiles, who live with unbridled physical force. A meat eater must kill the other to feed himself, so he must situate himself in a position of unscrupulous domination.

When all is said and done, if religion still finds grace in my eyes, it is because of its representatives. Francis of Assisi, naturally, is close to my heart. This lover of divine creation chose a life of destitution and spoke to birds. When I had the chance to read about the life of Saint Francis, I was struck by his pivotal choice, his radical decision to leave everything behind. He came from a wealthy Italian merchant family, but when he received a revelation, the next day he stripped himself naked saying, "Now, I no longer want anything material." He put on a tunic, tied it with a rope around his waist, and got rid of all of his beautiful clothing. He lived barefoot, close to nature and animals. One day, he went to the small city of Gubbio, where the inhabitants were afraid of a wolf roaming the area. Francis went to see the animal to make peace with it and then returned to the city accompanied by the wolf. This story of speaking with an animal, the reconnection between man and nature, is magnificent. Saint Francis of Assisi spoke about mercy for all things. This saint is a spiritual role model for me because the idea of simplicity and forgetting the self to give something to others solidifies the path I have chosen. Everything I had that was most precious was sold at auction to benefit my foundation. I find it reassuring that even the most beautiful things can be transformed, that they don't have to lie in a safe forever. The abandon of the material for the spiritual is the best path toward wisdom. All the more so if the sage is escorted by animals! Francis of Assisi conveyed a spirituality of compassion, without any distinction between the species, and this is why he is the patron saint of the animal cause, as well as my guide. On the other hand, I wouldn't go so far as walking on the bridge at La Madrague wearing a handmade woolen habit.

My exchanges with religious leaders have always been hit or miss, depending on the person. I had the pleasure of meeting John Paul II in 1995. I had been dispatched as a spokesperson by several animal protection organizations to make the trip to the Vatican. I remember a warm man; a gentle, benevolent, and charming representative of the faith. During a public audience, I asked him to think about animal suffering in the world, and to pass on a message so that men would no longer abuse their power over them, whether for self-interest or for profit. The pope bowed his head and said to me, "*Si, sì, ci penso io, ci penso.*" The meeting was public, and I didn't have very much time to speak, but he took my hands and looked into my eyes. I felt something powerful pass between us. He didn't seem to be working on his image, like so many official figures; he was inside himself, not performing a show. In a few seconds, I was able to recognize in John Paul II the depth I search for so often in my relationships with the human Other.

My relationship with Pope Francis is more complicated. There is a great deal of misunderstanding between us, especially because our exchanges have never been direct, which muddles things a little bit more. One of his first encyclical letters as the Supreme Pontiff, *Laudato si'* in 2015, made explicit reference to the song of Saint Francis of Assisi, "Laudato si', mi'Signore" ("Praise be to you, my Lord"). The pope's text was a hymn to creation and an alarm bell, warning people to protect it.

So for two years, I wrote him on October 4, the Feast of Saint Francis of Assisi. I suggested that he take advantage of the great symbolism of the name he had chosen and dedicate a day to animals. In reply, I received only a letter from an associate thanking me for my note. So I wrote him again. In vain. The year after, once again I wrote him a short letter reminding him that he had never acknowledged the two before. An emissary then informed me in person that Pope Francis preferred to take care of the cause of men before that of animals and that he disagreed with my political stance. I was shocked and hopeless. It is true that in my letter I had expressed how astonished I was that he was in favor of Muslim immigration, to the detriment of Christians in the Middle East who were in grave danger.[17] I believe this is what interfered with our potential dialogue. But I thought that Francis was above all of that. If he, too, is politicized, if he allows his personal considerations to be put above a humane reality, then to me he seems biased. Pope Francis's compassion is centered on humans, I understand that, but respect for animals is revealing about the rapport that those humans maintain with all forms of earthly life. I am speaking to him about respect for the creation and creatures of God, and he hands me back this unbearable idea of hierarchies between beings! These exchanges were brought to a close by a letter from the pope in October 2017, when he wrote me and included these words: "The heart is unique, and the same misery that leads us to mistreat an animal will not wait long before manifesting itself in our relationships with other people." I regret that these thoughts were not shared more widely.

I have never had the opportunity to meet with Jewish leaders concerning ritual slaughter. I have requested an audience with the Chief Rabbi of France several times, but I have always been refused. I want to clarify something here: I have no problem with food that is kosher for Jews and halal for Muslims as long as this dictate does not require the suffering of an animal having its throat cut. Technically, ritual slaughter in France cannot be performed unless it is in a slaughterhouse by slaughtermen authorized by recognized religious organizations.[18] On February

17 Letter from Brigitte Bardot to Pope Francis, September 28, 2017.
18 Legislation concerning ritual slaughter (source OABA website):
Ritual slaughter can only be performed in a slaughterhouse. Ignoring this requirement

11, 2004, I met with Dalil Boubakeur and the Grand Mufti at the Grande Mosquée de Paris to discuss halal meat and religious celebrations like Eid-al-Kebir that include animal sacrifice. This meeting was one of the most important of my life, first because I was immersing myself for a few hours in a culture I was unfamiliar with, and second because I had the feeling that millions of animal lives were depending on this moment. My aim was to convince the rector of the merits of electronarcosis, a method of stunning the animal without killing him so that the throat can be cut without pain during ritual sacrifices. Islam orders that an animal be alive at the time of the bleeding; I needed to prove that my suggestion had been rigorously researched and was sound. I explained that I understood this rule and thought that we could come to a place of understanding between religious tradition and animal respect. A sheep, for example, could still have his throat cut while alive, and the Muslim ritual for halal meat wouldn't be disrupted in the slightest. This is what I explained to

---

exposes the person performing the slaughter and the individual ordering it to a criminal sentence of six months in prison and 15,000 € in fines (article L.237-2 I of the rural code). Those who make available their premises, land, installations, material, or equipment for the purposes of a ritual slaughter outside of a slaughterhouse are committing a fourth class minor offense: art. R. 215-8 II . C. rural.

a. Ritual slaughter cannot be performed except by authorized slaughtermen. The slaughtermen must be authorized by recognized religious organizations: The Grande Mosquée de Paris, the Mosquée de Lyon, and the Mosquée of Évry for Muslim ritual slaughter; The Great Rabbinat for Jewish ritual slaughter. All ritual slaughter performed by a person other than an authorized slaughterman constitutes a fourth class minor offense: art. R. 215-8 II 10° C. rural. Every slaughterman must be able to prove his authorization to perform ritual slaughters to avoid receiving a third class fine: art. R. 215-8 III C. rural.

b. Animals must be immobilized before and during their bleeding. If intoxication of the animal is not required before putting them to death, article R. 214-74 C. rural nevertheless requires that bovine, ovine, and caprine species be immobilized by a mechanical procedure (which excludes all manual holding or the use of ties). This mechanical holding must precede the bleeding and must be maintained during the bleeding until the death of the animal. If these conditions are not adhered to, a fourth class contravention is imposed: art. R. 215-8 II 4° C. rural.

Dalil Boubakeur, who listened to me kindly and very attentively. His intelligence and his great faith led him to understand my request, which he accepted right away, as did the Mufti who accompanied him and who had my words translated for him by the rector. The two men spoke to each other, and I stood before them in tears. They agreed with the principle of bleeding an unconscious animal because the Quran did not forbid it. That day, I was greatly comforted by the thought that no matter what religion we belong to, the language of compassion belongs to everyone, an idea that would continue to be confirmed to me by the numerous other exchanges I would have with Dalil Boubakeur, for we stayed in touch for a long time via letters and telephone calls.

After our discussion on February 11, 2004, Dalil Boubakeur gathered the press in a large room in the Grande Mosquée de Paris. He announced to the journalists that he agreed with the principle of stunning animals before throat-cutting, and that it would now be up to the State to put it into law. This was a tremendous moment of relief, and I left with my heart more at ease than ever.

But this peace was short-lived, because these good intentions did not lead to any action, political or otherwise. On October 5, 2005, I finally obtained an interview with Nicolas Sarkozy, at the time minister of the interior and responsible for religious affairs. I poured my heart out to him, insisting that French law should follow our advice and make electronarcosis required in all slaughter situations and that it was time to do away with exemptions concerning ritual slaughter in France. Nicolas Sarkozy looked me straight in the eye and assured me that he would bring the Muslim leaders together and that the debate would be decided within eight days. As I write these lines, 4,046 days later, the throats of fully conscious animals are still being sliced open. Our secular country is one of the last European states that gives religious slaughtermen special permission to cut animal throats in slaughterhouses while the animals are still conscious. The problem is that the frantic rhythm in the slaughter lines forces them to slice the animals open haphazardly, causing failed attempts, animals being eviscerated while still living, etc. Austria forbids throat-cutting while an animal is conscious, without exemption, and the same is true for Denmark, Estonia, Finland, Greece, Iceland, Norway (outside EU), the Netherlands, Sweden, and Switzerland (outside EU). In Luxembourg, the Minister of Agriculture has the authority to grant exemptions, but so far this has never been done. Finally, the Belgian ban on slaughtering animals without stunning is set for June 2018 in Wallonia and September 2019 in Flanders.

Tradition
Ah, tradition: the classic excuse used by the very worst executioners, murderers, and all those indifferent to animal suffering. A lazy fable referred to by commentators who don't dare criticize a cruel cultural practice if it involves ancestral customs. This inertia is scandalous. This laissez-faire approach gives the defenders of these traditions an unassailable license to kill. That kind of tradition is an insult to the idea of progress that humans boast so much about.

EATING A DISEASED LIVER: IS THAT TRADITION?
France deserves special mention in this tableau of the unthinkable with one of its national "pride and joys," and an item inscribed into the cultural and gastronomic heritage of our country: foie gras. The creation of this festive dish in reality hides an abominable suffering. Geese and ducks are force-fed until they contract a liver disease comparable to cirrhosis: hepatic steatosis. The birds are overfed, twice a day, and are totally immobilized so that only their necks and beaks can be seen. Then

they are intubated with a hose that is placed down their esophagus. The creatures are stuffed with grains, corn, and a porridge filled with the lipids necessary for fattening up. What they gulp down is the equivalent of forty-four pounds of pasta per day for a human being. And when their liver reaches a volume ten times greater than normal, the web-footed birds are so fat they can hardly walk. Tables at the most luxurious French restaurants and family New Year's Eve dinners are riddled with this product, which is nothing but a tortured liver. The detention conditions and force-feeding techniques that cause injury and trauma in order to enlarge the liver are so damaging that no goose or duck could survive them. Foie gras is a disease that idiots enjoy.

In January 2016, the foundation supported a law proposed by Députée Laurence Abeille to the Assemblée Nationale that would ban force-feeding. Among the supporters of this cause was professor and animal defender Donald M. Broom, who came to present a scientific report detailing the harmful consequences of force-feeding on ducks and geese.

Also present at this conference were Michel Vandenbosch, the president of the Belgian organization Global Action in the Interest of Animals (GAIA) and Christophe Marie from my foundation who presented the results of an IFOP survey. In response to the question "Knowing that alternatives exist, would you be in favor of banning force-feeding for the production of foie gras?" seventy percent of French people responded "YES."[19]

This is the paradox of tradition: when real people are asked, and not the lobbyists and activists for one cause or another, we realize that customs involving animal suffering are considered archaic and outdated by the public.

---

19 IFOP survey for the Fondation Brigitte Bardot, "Les Français et la pratique du gavage," June 2016. http://ifop.fr/media/poll/3274-1- study_file.pdf.

TORTURING A BULL IN AN ARENA: IS THAT TRADITION?

Ritual slaughter is not the only battle in which exemptions allow animal torture to take place. In fact, it is thanks to these special dispensations that bullfighting, after having been illegal for a century up until 1950, is now enjoying an exceptional revival in France. The penal code condemns grave abuses and acts of cruelty toward an animal,[20] but these stipulations do not concern bullfights and "uninterrupted local traditions."

As long as a tradition is ancient, the enjoyment of a sadistic audience—one thirsty for blood, excited by the rods cutting into the bull's muscles, intoxicated by his faltering breaths as the banderillas are planted in his back or thoracic cage, causing unbearable internal hemorrhaging—is completely justified.

The tradition of bullfighting stimulates human cruelty.

The debate around this bull sacrifice is unending. In July 2016, however, we received a bit of hope: bullfighting was finally removed from the intangible heritage list in France; it was no longer an untouchable sanctuary. The places in France where this spectacle is still tolerated today are located between the Pays d'Arles and the Basque Country, between Provence and the Mediterranean, between the Pyrenees and Gascogne, Landes, and Languedoc. In Spain, the outlawing of bullfighting in Catalonia was later retracted. My foundation is obviously very present in the battle against this sadistic tradition. In 2011, we led a demonstration in the Rodilhan arenas in the Gard region to try and prevent six young cows from being put to death. The activists formed a peaceful circle in the middle of the track. They were horribly beaten by the *aficionados*. In 2013, we coorganized a similar protest in Rion-des-Landes. Christophe

---

20 Article 521-1: "The act, public or not, of committing violent or sexual abuses or acts of cruelty toward a domestic or tamed animal or an animal held in captivity is punishable by two years in prison and 30,000 €."

Marie, who in both of these cases was among the activists who jumped into the arena, was given a heavy sentence. This, to me, is a flagrant injustice; the guilty ones who are torturing an animal to death for the pleasure of a few perverts are given free rein by politicians and the justice system, while those opposed to these circus acts are dragged before a judge. It's disheartening.

I myself attended a bullfight in Seville while I was filming *The Female*.[21] Already sensitive to the animal cause, I had been encouraged to attend this kind of spectacle to know more about the injustices I was already condemning in my heart and soul. The entire show was an ordeal; for the murdered bull, of course, but also for me. I had the urge to vomit, the kind of nausea that comes up into your throat and gives you cold sweats. My hands were clammy; I was horrified, scandalized, and incapable of saving the animal who was being stabbed in front of my eyes. During this long "game" of torture, which then became an execution, I felt more than ever like an accomplice to cruelty. I have never been as ashamed of myself as I was in that moment. Like a worthless and disgusting person, I was quietly sitting in the stands of this arena, drowning in a hysterical crowd shouting out "*bravo!*" and "*vivat!*" as if they were greeting and cheering on a hero. During this interminable bullfight, I felt once again the difference that has always set me apart from other people: I am decidedly *not* adapted to this world, one that contemplates the agony of a living being with pleasure. Observing the body of the bull, who had been very much alive, majestic, and proud twenty minutes before, I felt like going down and kneeling on the soiled sand to take him in my arms. The bloodied body, perforated all over by the banderillas, was dragged by horses until it disappeared into the wings. Watching this innocent martyr leaving his execution site wounded me forever. I had

---

21 *The Female*, directed by Julien Duvivier, 1959.

lost a great deal of my innocence. My friend had been right, though: I needed to witness a tragedy like this to feed the rage, the force, the antibullfight activism that is still mine today.

KILLING FOR LEISURE: IS THAT TRADITION?

How do you legalize a murder? By calling it a "hunt." With this title, killing can be done for fun; killing can be a leisure activity. In France, hunting is considered entertainment, a recreational sport. And for me, this is a battle that has been going on for ages.

Hunters have made me sick since very early in my life. This nausea has led to multiple confrontations, very often in a social context. In *Initiales B.B.*, I tell the story of a hunting party I participated in with Vadim early in our marriage. He had been sent by *Paris Match* to do a report at the home of the Vicomtesse de Luynes. He saw it as a chance to socialize with people he considered "charming." I was very young, but all of this already bored me no end. Not to mention that the occasion bringing us all together that day was beyond morbid. I went into the forest while a stag hunt was underway. All around, I heard the horns, the horses galloping, and the dogs barking. I remember thinking that I needed to find a way to divert the hunters' attention so that they would make me their target and not the poor animal they were hounding. I told myself, "If I start running, they'll think it's me, that I'm the animal they're supposed to hit." I cried my eyes out against a tree trunk, pleading for the people of the forest to be left in peace. In vain. That night, a stag was lying in a pool of blood in the courtyard. Furious, and feeling as if I myself had been stripped of the life that had been taken from such a beautiful animal, I fled that house of terror.

When I was forty-four, Yvonne, my friend and neighbor at Bazoches, invited me to a dinner with, among others, Nelly Guerlain and her husband, whom I didn't know. It was one of those soirees where everyone is impeccably dressed and the guests exchange small talk . . . that is, until

Madame Guerlain began sharing with us her hunting misfortunes. She told us that she had quite a time dislodging a stag who had taken refuge in a pond during one of her most recent stag hunts. She had been forced to go into the icy water herself and stab him with a knife while her dog tore him limb from limb. As a result, poor Nelly Guerlain had caught the flu. Unable to listen to this horror, I politely asked that we change the subject, but Nelly Guerlain continued, this time regaling us with her impressive pheasant kill count. In the face of this indifference, or perhaps it was provocation, I stood up, dumbfounded and trembling with rage, and snapped, "Madame, do you know what the worst thing about a Guerlain woman is? That no one can stand her!" Even after this retort, which would forge my reputation, I found the situation absolutely intolerable. Not to mention that the atrocities being committed under my nose were the work of a woman. I know the base predator instincts that can drive men, but when women are involved, I trip over my total incomprehension. It was the same with the Dessange couple. Jacques was my hairdresser during my great period as a star, and I became friends with his wife. But these two were regular hunters. So, as time passed and the animal cause took on greater and greater prominence in my life, a distance was created in our friendship. I started by refusing to go to their home on hunting days, then I eventually stopped spending weekends at their house, which was decorated exclusively with game trophies. We were often at odds because I could not accept this kind of cruelty. I told them they were being unbearably cowardly by hunting, and that I didn't understand how a person could take pleasure in killing a magnificent and perfectly healthy animal who had to be lured out with tricks, beaters, and excited dogs . . . and they thought I was an idiot. My defense of animals and the continuation of this relationship became irreconcilable.

Hunting involves a great deal of cowardice. I have never met beings more fainthearted than hunters. These are the kind of people who took my dogs one day when they had run off across a field at Bazoches. The bodies of my companions were never found. It was also a hunter who turned a gun on me one day because I had put myself between him and a wild boar who had taken refuge at my home in Saint-Tropez. This man, whose vulgarity was equaled only by his hostility, threatened me, saying, "I have two cartridges in my rifle, and if you keep me from killing this wild boar, there's one for you and one for him." It didn't take long for me to threaten him myself: "So shoot!"

This long battle against hunting reached its climax in Saint-Tropez of all places, on that cruel day of June 4, 1994, when I felt completely betrayed by the town I loved so much. Saint-Tropez, a city associated with the name of Brigitte Bardot, Saint-Tropez, so tied to my animal mission, had agreed to host a convention for seven hundred hunters. I took it as a provocation. Especially because this town of pleasure and tourism had never been a hunting area, and any game animals who had lived there would have cleared off long ago, threatened by the extension of building zones. But this bitterness ended up putting me in danger. Supported by hundreds of other activists, I hurled myself against the fence surrounding this gathering of hunters. The crowd was so enthusiastic that I became pinned against the barrier. I was being smothered. On the other side, men were looking at me and mocking me. I managed to free myself and hid in a boutique.

The joy of killing a defenseless animal has mutated enormously in recent years. Hunters are no longer armed with little shooters; they are equipped with a veritable arsenal worthy of the battlefield. This is what makes me believe, more than ever, that today I am in a war against them. My enemies are the traditional "Sunday" hunters, carriers of a license to kill, defenders of a lifestyle that allows them to satisfy their sadistic desires. My enemies are the trap setters: the people putting down little branches coated in glue that condemn birds to die with their feet or feathers stuck to them, or the people hunting lapwings by attaching strings to their tails. My enemies are the inheritors of the vile monarchist tradition that is the fox hunt, a symbol of the ancien régime. The underground portion of the hunt is particularly cruel: the animal is pushed into its den by the dogs before it is dislodged with metal clamps. The tradition of the foxhunt was abolished in England in 2004, and one year later my foundation initiated a similar proposal for France. The text submitted to the Assemblée Nationale by Jean Marsaudon was shelved.[22]

There was a great stir in the fall of 2017, when a stag was cruelly killed on private property in the Oise region. I was shocked and revolted by this "murder." There is no other word for what happened to this poor deer, who had taken refuge in someone's yard after five hours of deadly pursuit. How can something so shameful be accepted? How can this hunt from the Middle Ages not be abolished when the only people who practice it are sadists in a fake and inhumane aristocracy? The disgusting tradition known as *droit de suite*, or right to follow, authorizes the bloodthirsty idiot of a hunter to pursue a wounded stag anywhere in order to kill him, either with a dagger or by any other method. Several petitions have been launched for the abolition of foxhunting, and my foundation, following the example of SPA, has filed a complaint citing "grave abuses and acts of cruelty" toward a wild animal. The stag is a noble animal, majestically crowned with antlers, an enchanting and royal animal, a powerful animal, so superior to the self-indulgent people pretending to be royalty who try and chase him down. I hope with all my heart that the murder of Compiègne will finally make the government aware of the horror that this "leisure" represents so that foxhunting can be abolished once and for all, for it is one of the great shames of France.

---

22 UMP député from Essonne who died in 2008.

Astonishingly, in our country, hunting benefits from an enormous amount of complacency on the part of the general public. It is the legacy of a rural past, and yet it is one of the traditions that carries out the greatest injustices toward animals. My foundation kept count: thirty-one million animals are killed each year, and the hunting season covers nine months out of twelve. Animals have only three months of respite each year, the mating period. The species that are most targeted are wood pigeons, pheasants, thrushes, hares and wild rabbits, partridges, woodcocks, and wild boars. Attacking a domestic animal in our territory is illegal, but it is entirely permissible to mistreat a wild animal. My foundation and I are asking that wild animals be recognized as sentient beings and, as a result, that atrocities toward them be punishable by the law.

Most of the time, a hunt is just a stupid trophy race. In recent times, animal protection organizations have witnessed the development of perverted safaris on certain African reserves: endangered species hunts. You may be thinking of the sadly famous Cecil the lion, killed in 2015 by Walter Palmer, an American hunter without scruples. Unfortunately, this was not an isolated incident, and my foundation was quick to condemn this scandal, which we hope will take on global proportions before it is too late. The factors driving this trophy hunt are the corruption of certain members of nature reserves, the moneymaking potential these threatened animals possess, and the leisure time of wealthy hunters. Several specialized agencies even offer to organize these murderous raids, providing clients with guides to drive them around while they hunt lions, leopards, warthogs, elephants, rhinos, giraffes, gazelles, and crocodiles. We forwarded a petition to Ban Ki-moon, secretary-general of the United Nations, accompanied by a letter written by me in which I condemn what should be considered premeditated murders, as the targets are already known and easy to shoot.

Added to this shameful practice is canned hunting, which is developing steadily in South Africa, where thousands of wild animals are raised to be killed by hunters, always with the complicity of various agencies offering rich collectors the possibility to satiate their desire for trophies.

So, when people ask me why I have such a ferocious hatred for hunters, I have only one answer: because they are murderers. Hunting, a traditional leisure activity, is merely the morbid enjoyment of spilling blood. I am thinking in particular about the Grind. Every year, unbearable images come to us from the Faroe Islands, a Danish territory, where the inhabitants indulge in a tradition as bloody as it is useless. The process is particularly vicious: fishermen encircle one hundred black pilot whales, a rare kind of dolphin, to funnel them into a bay. Pushed into a corner, the cetaceans are in the trap. The participants in this marine killing spree have nothing left to do but massacre the poor mammals. Males, females, and babies are knifed and stabbed to death. This carnage lasts for a few hours, then the corpses of the dolphins are abandoned, lying on the beach next to a sea of blood. The participants leave the scene of the crime, satisfied that they have upheld the tradition, leaving behind the murdered bodies that will eventually rot in undersea trenches, as ethnologist François-Xavier Pelletier revealed during his "Stop the Grind" mission led by Sea Shepherd in 2010 and financed completely by my foundation.

IS IT STILL TRADITION?

The calendar is sprinkled with dates that are overshadowed by inconceivable killings. Tradition can make any kind of cruelty seem acceptable because it justifies in itself what is immoral. Every June 21, I am horrified. The dogmeat festival in Yulin, China, hurts my body and heart. Despite the protests of animal protection organizations around the world, this "celebration" is held every year: a day when thousands of dogs and cats are beaten to death and boiled alive by butchers who then carve the pieces of meat. The cut-up yellowed dog carcasses pay testament to the punishment inflicted upon these poor creatures: their tails are stiffened, and their jaws are gaping wide. This is the worst persecution that I fight against with my foundation. Seeing dogs and cats put through this kind of torment makes me furious; it's just too atrocious, too inhumane, too foul.

Spain is a country particularly rich in shameful traditions. One of them, involving Spanish greyhounds, has been among my foundation's great battles for the past fifteen years. Two breeds of dogs called *galgos* and *podencos* are used for hunting and races. Then, when the dogs become unusable, their owners get rid of them by hanging them from trees or drowning them in wells, spraying them with acid, and puncturing their eyes. Another tradition in Valencia has people douse a bull's horns with tar and gasoline and then set them on fire. The panicked animal flees into the crowd where people throw bricks and stones at him. In Extremadura, there is another "celebration" in which a donkey crosses a village to be stoned to death.

In all of these instances of tradition, we humans are waiting to see force and human virility triumph over the animal. It represents the victory of power over vulnerability. People who admire these legacies from another age are showing us a darker side of man, the side of him that finds morbid enjoyment in inflicted suffering, and also reveal a hatred of the other that is hidden away within him. On the pretext of allowing a culture to express itself, in truth these traditions of blood only foster an enthusiasm for all that is morbid and callous, and they are the symbol of the profound depths of human perversity.

The Revenge of Mistreated Animals

The reality of animal mistreatment is concealed, so well hidden that we forget that it should be considered one of the great battles for the emancipation of living beings. Sometimes, though, and in an indirect way, animals are able to remind us how they are being treated.

We do not realize it, because it is a subject that is too often neglected, but the greatest epidemiological scandals of today are linked to food consumption. Oh, yes . . . all of those factory farms are the perfect home for viruses!

We started hearing people talk about animal diseases and threats to humans in the nineties with the famous "mad cow disease." This infection was caused by the use of bonemeal in the food given to cows. To make up for the lack of protein in the animals themselves, they were engorged with bonemeals containing pieces of meat, carcasses, and bovine bodies.

Then, in the early 2000s, H5N1, or avian flu, arrived. This time, chickens, turkeys, ducks, and geese were affected. The contact between living animals and dead bodies, infected fecal matter, and rodents was the cause of the problem. The same was true for the aphthous fever, or foot-and-mouth disease, in pigs, goats, and sheep.

In each of these cases, humans were only very rarely infected. This is not the case for the diseases I will mention next.

The changes in food consumption and the multiplication of farms and, therefore, bacteria have ushered in diseases like listeria and salmonella that are caused by the consumption of infected foods and animal proteins. The infamous Creutzfeldt-Jakob disease also involves the ingestion of contaminated meat. Eggs contaminated with fipronil, an antiparasitic used on factory farms, pose yet another risk to human health.

I have not even mentioned the other issues that are beyond our ability to measure: the explosion of allergies, asthma, and wild growth rates in children and adolescents fed hormone-treated chicken. Kids are eating hamburgers made from a cow who had been genetically altered by growth hormones. The result: girls are starting puberty at ever-younger ages, and pediatricians and physicians are confronted with diseases they haven't seen before, including a variety of autoimmune diseases.

Bad food makes people ill and causes deformations. Meat and animal products that have been produced in an unnatural way have created what are being called *zoonotic diseases*, infections that are transmissible from animals to humans. The link between industrial farming and these epidemics is obvious.

I have a profound disgust for the time period I am living in. We are poisoning animals who are supposed to provide healthy nourishment for humans, keeping them alive with the help of disgusting substances, and when we realize that we have created creatures who are abnormal and dangerous for humans, we get rid of them by euthanizing them, burning them, and wiping them off the map. And then we start over somewhere else with other methods and other products that will give birth to other Frankensteins. The eggs contaminated with fipronil were thrown out by the billions the moment the problem was detected. What a waste, what tremendous waste. When a chicken lays an egg, it is an effort for her; the process of successfully giving birth takes a long time. To no longer appreciate that, to simply produce and destroy for no reason, is the scandal of our century.

Feeding animals with dead things and feeding humans with animals who have been fed to their death: this is the suicide of humanity. And the death of ethics. We complain about athletes doping during competitions, but consumers today have every opportunity to dope themselves with any animal product they wish. When you have to give bonemeal, antiparasitics, and antibiotics to animals and fish, there is obviously a huge problem. And then, those same animals end up poisoning the very people who forced them to eat that disgusting food.

If all of this seems complicated to you, if it is difficult for you to untangle what is true from what is false or to understand the reality of epidemics and zoonotic diseases, think for a moment about the staple food of animals intended for consumption: grass. That's all, just grass.

"Animal disease," which will affect more and more humans in the future, is a kind of revenge on the part of animals against the sorcerer's apprentice that man has become. As Jane Goodall very accurately put it, "We are what we eat."[23]

Vegetarianism

I have not eaten meat in over forty years, but I think I was always a vegetarian. I was always horrified by meat: Maman would pinch my nose to make me swallow it. I saw the blood, the red and juicy flesh, and I was disgusted. I was always aware that eating meat was eating a dead creature. And it's not so very different from a kind of cannibalism.

Vegetarianism is an incremental journey, but in general it is irreversible. When I was an actress, I was constantly surrounded by people eating meat, and in the cinema cafeterias or restaurants I went to, I was always offered dishes composed solely of chicken, beef, or some other meat. I would eat as little of it as possible. Then I started to become concerned about animal life and, naturally, the conditions in the slaughterhouses. As time went by, this refusal of meat became important to me,

---

23 Title of the very beautiful book by Jane Goodall, published by Actes Sud in 2012.

until the day when it became permanent. I could no longer separate what was on my plate from what I had seen. This is how I came to my decision.

Forty years ago, there were still very few vegetarians in our society, and I was looked at as if I were a strange creature . . . the way I'd always been looked at, in fact. Vegetarianism was considered a slightly sectarian practice, something gurus would do. Fortunately, this is no longer the case, and today, veganism—the refusal of all products derived from the exploitation of animals—is also practiced. I'm not a vegan, as I have already said, because I still enjoy honey, eggs, cream, and cheese. It does not bother me to consume these foods, because I see it as an exchange with animals: I offer them my protection, my care, my love, and they give me a little milk and a few eggs. I am not about consumption, but moderation, because I know the gift that nature is giving me through these products.

The world might eventually become vegetarian, though, because soon killing in order to eat will no longer make any sense. This idea is spreading: it is more of an awareness than a fashionable way of thinking. I'm well aware that the transition will be long; our culture is so marked by farming, and our gastronomy is based on animal proteins. I often hear other solutions that are neither here nor there: if farming becomes clean again, and if slaughter methods are regulated, the life and death of animals will be healthier and therefore acceptable. In other words: if man no longer makes animals suffer in order to eat them, it will be tolerable to kill them. This is a compromise I cannot accept. For my eighty-third birthday, I was given vegan sausages made with vegetable proteins, soy, and wheat. They looked just like meat sausages, without containing the real thing, and yet the effect on me was the same. Calling these alternative foods by the same name and forming them into the same shape reminds me too much of the world of meat. Refusing to eat animal flesh is not just refusing a taste, it is also rejecting a system that exploits the other for its own needs.

The flesh swallowed by a human being becomes his own flesh. If he eats a tortured animal, he will be nourishing himself with a painful death and, without realizing it, he will be unable to digest it. I was born in 1934, and I come from a time when meat was a rare product that was expensive and respected. Today, it is simply a piece of common flesh, ugly and easy to throw away. It is now ordinary to eat meat and dairy products, even though this should not be the case. The way that meat is produced today poses a moral problem. It can make us sick, it infringes upon the dignity of billions of animals each year, and it contributes to global warming because of the industrialization of farming. The public is beginning to understand all of this, and these values should show up in their home refrigerators. Before being collectively responsible, we must be individually responsible.

Emotion and Reason

People are starting to think and are no longer blind consumers. I'm satisfied to see that with the rise of social networks, a part of the public is becoming aware of numerous cases of animal suffering and denouncing them. When people are shown images of cruelty, I'm convinced that this changes their mentality. When they are faced with screaming animals dying in slaughter centers, for example, they have no choice but to cry out against this injustice. A public that doesn't imagine or visualize something taking place can't realize that it is actually happening. It can't tell whether or not we are simply sticking our nose where we shouldn't be. People will say, "It's always been like this," or, "I like animals, I would never hurt one, but I like to eat steak!" How many times have I heard that!

This naiveté comes from an ensemble of things: a lack of information, ignorance, and a submission to consumer society. Few people make the connection between the little lamb they pet the day before and the meat they will eat the following day. The meat lobbies make sure to show ads that incite the public to eat their products. The propaganda is positive: the pig is happy to be killed and to give you something to eat. We are shown joyful little animals, made to look nice to promote the brand. As a result, even if a consumer is disgusted one day, the next day he or she will forget about it and think about something else.

This is human nature. This is what our society is like: it is better to be reasonable than to be emotional. This is why things are having a hard time getting moving, because emotion is not taking precedence over reason, because the man in the street is not the one making the laws. The vast majority of people no longer want animals to be seen as objects. Alas, animals are far, far too connected to economic interests that none of us are even aware of. Animals aren't slaves for no reason. They're slaves because they help turn a profit. Imagine for a moment a society without wool, without leather, without milk, eggs, or meat, without medications, without cosmetics, without entertainment. Can you? No. But can we imagine one without an animal presence? Yes. This is why the slave-animal model works for everybody. It is so convenient to exploit someone who suffers in silence. I have often read that we cannot give animals rights because they cannot be given any responsibilities. What nonsense! Are we waiting for animals to demonstrate reasoning, for them to speak, before we pay attention to them? Are we waiting for them to blow us away with their abilities before we respect them and stop bullying them? I don't believe that animal protection will succeed solely through discovery, science, or the institution of laws recognizing the rights of animals. Those are good things, but they will never be enough.

Animal protection will succeed because of virtues that are dying out in humans: compassion and love.

This is why I prefer emotion to reason. I am often criticized for my strong feelings, my rages, and my words, but they are simply translating the pain I feel for mistreated animals. My pain is equal to the enormity of our task. Equal to all of this violence, and equal to the inertia that surrounds it.

Taking care of animals is not a vain occupation. It's not the pastime of a former actress who likes petting her cat. It is a veritable battle to change how people look at things so that I will no longer have to hear this sentence, so fraught with meaning: "It's just an animal." The animal of today is a slave to men, and nothing else is more important to me than his liberation, seeing him freed from his chains, freed from the unhealthy perceptions people have of him, and seeing him shine in his splendor.

4

My Dream as an Inheritance

Humane Humans

My battle was born out of a dream, a wild imagination, a desire for justice. It was born out of an ideal, though I was someone who always kept my feet on the ground.

A dream only had meaning if it was realized, and so I always searched for an alternative, a choice other than the one I had been given. When I was a child, I escaped into my fantasies: I sometimes dreamed of being a principal dancer, spending my days at the Paris Opera; other times, I dreamed of being a shepherdess. I missed the countryside so much that it had become my dream world, an earthly paradise filled with forest animals, fields of wheat, and rivers where wolves came to drink. I also dreamed of living on an African nature reserve, surrounded by elephants who would share a little of their wisdom with me.

I am still just as much of a dreamer today. My spirit drifts toward beautiful things and magnificent places, the products of my imagination. When I feed my pigeons on my terrace, I wonder what they can see with their small round eyes, what they are thinking about when they let themselves be carried through the sky.

My life became a dream for many people, though it often seemed like a nightmare to me. My destiny was centered around my image: a fantasy, glory, and power, all things that evaporate at the first sign of wind. I would have liked to have had magic powers, to move mountains and affect change. I am living proof that celebrity status offers nothing more than a prestige that is snuffed out when the artificial lights that once made it glow are turned off. In another life, I shone because of my beauty; yesterday it was because of the stances I took, and today it is because of a myth that I never wished to construct. Only my foundation is anchored in the hard ground of reality. But this doesn't give me any power. Power is not something we can hold firmly in our hands, like a magic wand. It is an ever-moving serpent that has its own interests, resources, and collusions. Unfortunately, power, as it is exerted today, tends more easily toward destruction than construction.

Being Brigitte Bardot does not give me any power.

All I am able to do is condemn what is wrong. Now and for always. And if a few habits from my former acting career have stayed with me, they are found in my ability to embody my battle. An actor exhibits, portrays a character, and creates a universe the audience can enter into. I have the power to put animal lives in the spotlight, to give value to their existence, and to invite people to refuse to accept unbearable truths. To make each person see the world through my eyes.

We all have the choice to behave as either the hero or the villain. This is why I have such a poor opinion of humanity. I cannot manage to justify how humans are able to let things stay the way they are and participate in such filthy practices involving both animals and themselves. When man is not at war, he hunts. He has a fundamental need to spill the blood of another living thing, to express his inner barbarian. Out of fear of death, out of fear of himself, the human being becomes a monster. He carries the yin and the yang within him, but because it's easier, certain people lose themselves in the negative. It's true that it's more difficult to cultivate the positive, but in the long term, it is more fulfilling.

My humanity is a continuous quest. To search elsewhere, farther, always deeper. I have burned the candle of my life at both ends, devoured my days, and dug out every possible opportunity from my existence. I have sublimated my person, destroyed my image. I have loved; always very much, and sometimes badly. I have reasoned and I have lost my mind. I have been adored and hated. I have wanted to live and to die. I have experienced everything. I have seen everything. So, what else is left for me apart from hope, the impossible dream, the superior desire to no longer see a humanity that murders others and kills itself? I am fighting without an army or armor, without a method, without questions, without rest. I am fighting for the unattainable, for a moment of peace and rest for animals.

It is time. Time to offer my dream as an inheritance, to lift the animal condition and inscribe it among the other great humanist battles that are the pride of my species. So that the animal will no longer be the object of man's domination, but a whole and complete individual. So that the animal will no longer be an easy victim for inhumane humans, but instead a member of an animal world and in possession of a newfound animality.

Animal Individuals

Animals are individuals, too. Every single one of them. They exist and they live. They are concrete individuals with a past, a present, and a future. The animal has always been seen as a machine acting purely out of instinct while man was developing his reflective skills. A person only needs to immerse him- or herself in the animal universe for a few days to realize that this partitioning of the world is inaccurate. Just like humans, animals are part of a species, but each individual is singular and unique from the others. One dog never resembles another dog. To my mare, I am not a representative of my species, which we call humans, I am Brigitte, the woman she shares her days with. And in the same way, I never judge an animal as a function of the group to which he belongs. Depending on the existence he has been given and the way he was raised, one cat can be very different from another.

Every animal has a personality, a temperament, and, of course, an awareness of himself. The classic scientific test to know whether an animal is capable of self-recognition is to put him in front of a mirror. How miraculous! Dolphins, pigs, elephants, and monkeys recognize themselves. Baby humans, by the way, are unable to do this before the age of a year and a half. Animals know they are alive and struggle to stay that way. They are capable of telling the difference between a slap and a caress. And their defiance toward their torturers is not the result of reflex or primary stimuli. Man does not have a monopoly on sensitivity, pain, and affection. People have told me stories about chimpanzees or baby rhinos who had been fed with a bottle and then released into the wild. Later, when the adult animals are reunited with their caregivers, they rush toward them. This is not a demonstration of instinct, it's a memory, fidelity. I could give you hundreds of examples in any species. Wolves recognize—in the blink of an eye—the women and men who have loved and protected them.

I don't like the word *intelligence*, because it is the symbol of a devastating human arrogance. It's not a word that we should stick on animals, because it doesn't mean anything, not even for humans. Animals' minds are obviously functioning at full capacity. If a monkey, dog, or parrot wants to eat a peanut that is stuck in a hole, he or she will find a way to get it out using any means necessary. And it is not instinct that orders them to pull on a rope to receive food, it is not something natural; it is the fruit of reflection. Animals all have a wealth of signals they use to express their joy, anger, surprise, or impatience. Why would we have exclusive rights to emotion? Why would we be the only holders of these riches that are the work of the heart and mind?

The only beings who enjoy a little more of our esteem are the great apes, because gorillas, orangutans, and chimpanzees are our cousins—our brothers, even. We have the same gestures for rocking a child, the same facial expressions, the same way of organizing a society or a family, and the same quarrels. If man has a greater regard for primates, it is because they resemble him. Man, therefore, has a need to compare himself and to find similarities with something in order to show it love and respect.

The majority of narrow-minded humans are waiting for us to prove that a pig is intelligent in order for them to consider him an individual, because human intelligence is being used as the point of reference. Well, the animal world is far richer than that and offers us a whole range of capacities, ingenuities, reflections, and wisdoms, depending on the species, of course, and on each animal's personality. In addition, it is not the intelligence of an individual that should engender our respect for it, it is its life and the mystery of possibilities that its existence holds.

For as long as I've had the good fortune to live constantly surrounded by animals, I have never stopped observing, not even for a second, the way they behave with one another. Their sense of fairness is unbelievable. This is certainly the case, of course, with mamas and their little ones, to whom they pass on their knowledge, and whom they invite slowly but surely to imitate them so that they can become responsible adults. It's also the case with elephants, who protect one of their own when he is in a dangerous situation by gathering together and surrounding him. I am also reminded of a video I was shown of a dog lying in the middle of the road, cars passing by without worrying whether he was dead or alive, until another dog comes along and uses his teeth to drag him by the nape of his neck off to the side. Animals stand in solidarity with one another, and with humans, too. This is easy to see if we briefly examine the relationship that human beings with disabilities have with the animals who accompany them. One might say that certain dogs are simply trained this way, to only obey orders. One might say that, but we should also admit that when a human finds himself in a dangerous situation, an animal will do all he can to rescue him. This capacity isn't related to instinct. It's an awareness, this is obvious.

Furthermore, the difference in language in no way proves that animals lack the capacity for reflection. Their communication is simply something that is not verbal. Pigeons know how to count, whales speak to one another with sounds, bees dance, chickens sympathize with one another, dogs utilize their sense of smell to recognize one another and sniff out certain human diseases, birds sing, and horses have all kinds of facial gestures to express their emotions. The same is true for monkeys.

It's only the predator in man that denies this diversity. It's only his dominating instinct that refuses to acknowledge the richness of the animal world, even though this acknowledgment takes nothing away from his humanity; it simply allows other life to express itself freely.

It's incredible to see to what extent an animal can very accurately perceive what he is, what surrounds him, and the means he has available to survive. This is why keeping a wild animal in captivity is a crime. A person would have to be blind to be unable to read the distress in a lion's eyes or in the constant pacing back and forth that is keeping him alive. I feel this despair myself, just as I feel the pain of a dog who has been beaten and mistreated. Animals who have been condemned to death know what is happening. In experimental laboratories, the eyes of the monkeys testify to a bottomless anguish. Without words, they plea; without crying out, they call for help.

The fact that they submit does not prove that they are unaware of what is going on. On the contrary, animals fight and fight as long as there is still time, and then when there is no longer any hope, they give up. They know, and understand quickly—more quickly than we do— when the only way out of their misery is death.

When all is said and done, what escapes many humans is an understanding of animals' vulnerability. Not their inferiority, but their vulnerability. What makes a brawny man different from a child is fragility. They have neither the same strength nor the same capacity for reflection. I believe that what separates man from animal is the same. Animals are condemned to silence and are unable to ask for our benevolence or demand rights for themselves. They are individuals without a voice and without defense. Like all of the most fragile beings, they deserve our attention and our protection. Our sensitivity should be joined with theirs. And give birth to a new ethics.

In Favor of an Animal Morality and Ethics

The animal is part of humanity's history. We think that, despite living side by side with them for years, we don't actually need them to live. Nothing could be further from the truth.

If I have agreed to write this final book, it is for two things: animal morality and ethics. These terms have always been what drives me. Morality, first and foremost. I would like us to recognize the difference between the good and evil that we do to animals, what is just and unjust, what is acceptable and what is not. And then ethics: we need to give animals a new place in our lives and in our thinking, and know that our actions have consequences for them.

More than anything, I want humans to feel responsible for animal lives. Once we know what animals perceive, sense, and suffer, we can no longer act as if we didn't know. Once we are conscious that they have concerns and notions of life and death, we cannot exploit their existence like pieces of equipment that are at our disposal. Once we have stopped ignoring our similarities and our differences, humans should accept that they are part of a whole ensemble of "living things" with animals. And finally, once we recognize animals' vulnerability, we will only have one source of shame: exploiting them, and only one objective: to protect them.

The way we look at animals needs to change. They have the right to be respected, not as things but as individuals, which is why all forms of animal exploitation should be abolished. This is the meaning of humanity's existence: to improve the rights of all living beings. I grew up in a world where a wife was her husband's property and children didn't have the right to express themselves. They have now been given their own place in society. I would like the evolution of humanity to now move on to improving the fate and the place of animals.

Showing regard for animals should start with a rejection of hypocrisy: people have a dog in their homes but have no qualms about a pig being sacrificed so they can eat ham. The meaning of ownership is very important when we possess or are accompanied by an animal. This is why my foundation is very concerned about the rights of pets, favoring adoptions and not purchases that increase demand for filthy trafficking. We are trying to transform the words people use when discussing this subject. I would like us to no longer hear about an animal's "owner," but instead the person who is "responsible for" an animal. Animals are entrusted to us, not given to us, and we have a duty to them. In 1993, we proposed a fifteen-point charter to the mayors of France that included suggestions about managing animal placements, paying people when they adopt an animal, creating a civil status for each individual, and even levying a tax on each birth in a breeding center or private home. The goal was to foster an understanding of the responsibilities involved in housing a domestic animal and to fight against trafficking and animal abandonment.

Respecting animals means being capable of putting ourselves in their place. We will be able to do this only if we admit that all living beings are endowed with sensitivity. Domestic animals as well as wild animals. This involves the justice system, of course, but also the educational system. School programs need to be reexamined to include classes about animals, nature, and man's place in it. Days dedicated to animals should also be created. This is what my foundation did with the Fête du monde animal, which we first celebrated in 1989 at the hippodrome in Vincennes in collaboration with the Mairie de Paris. It was a chance to invite all of the animal organizations together and to offer a large number of dogs and cats a chance to be adopted.

Human progress is about advancing the rights of those who are the most vulnerable. It's thinking about the consequences of our actions on others. It's putting ourselves in the place of the other when all is said and done. Sensitivity gives animals rights, and the natural tendency of the animal individual to stay alive gives him rights. If the value of animal life continues to be denied by men, this attitude will jeopardize humanity permanently. To such an extent that it will lose one of its greatest qualities: mercy.

In Favor of Effective Legal Protection

Animals do not yet have their own legal rights. Yes, they enjoy the status of "sentient beings" in Europe and France,[1] but this text is not a foolproof protection from the cruel everyday practices of hunting, slaughtering, farming, and "leisure" of all kinds. For example, the law condemns cruelty, but not where the force-feeding of geese, bullfighting, and cockfights are concerned.

The animal is "sentient" in writing but remains "material" in practice. A pet cat, a lamb in the slaughterhouse, or a mink from a farm remain objects of commerce and trade. Unfortunately, property and sentience don't mix. This qualifier doesn't mean anything; it's a bandage on top of a scar that is too deep, a bone that is thrown to animal organizations. It doesn't change anything that is happening.

Nevertheless, 2017 will always be known as a landmark year for animal protection. Thanks to the organization L214, which had openly criticized the sadistic actions of a man in an organic slaughterhouse in the Gard, this executioner was sentenced to eight months in prison with probation and six hundred euros in fines for "grave abuses" by the correctional court in Alès. That same year, a man who had tortured a little cat to death in Draguignan was sentenced to six months in prison. A criminal act against an animal being had finally been recognized. I hope that these two verdicts will establish a precedent, because it is a great step forward in caring for animals and a victory for all organizations. This shift in awareness at the judicial level is the result of a long effort

---

1 Article L214 of the rural code has stipulated since 1976 that "as a sentient being, every animal should be placed by its owner in conditions compatible with the biological needs of its species." Acts of cruelty became an offense in 1963. Farm animals have been considered sentient beings by the law since 1976. In Europe, the Treaty of Rome that spoke about "agricultural products and merchandise" was overridden by the Treaty of Amsterdam in 1997, which demanded "respect for animals as sentient creatures."

over the past few years, as well as, and perhaps most of all, the mounting public outcry on social media.

In Favor of France Becoming a Country for Animals

I am the most well-known French woman in the world, I believe, and my country is far from being avant-garde when it comes to animal protection. I continue to be a film legend in other countries, of course; items of clothing are made using my name, products in my likeness are handed out, and exhibitions are organized. The star I was is still praised in many circles. These international homages do not exclude my status as a protector of animals, though. Far from it. I know from the letters people write me that many of them have never even seen one of my films; the younger generations, born during and after the eighties, know me for my activism and my foundation. This is what leads me to believe that if I had left film in 1973 to simply enjoy my years of retirement at La Madrague, no one would have ever talked about me again. It's my battle that has sustained my popularity, my dedication to this cause that has given meaning to the adoration people still sometimes extend to me. I am also very aware of being a French "brand" that France has taken full advantage of. Charles de Gaulle used to say that I brought as much to my country as the Renault slogans, and John Wayne had the audacity to declare, "The only French words I know how to pronounce are Brigitte Bardot."

With all of this in mind, I wish that the country I have represented so often would honor itself by enlisting in the humanist battle for animals. I want this homeland of enlightenment, of progress and equality, this nation of the rights of man to become one for animals, as well. Many European countries today are ahead of us in animal protection, and I cannot explain the reasons for this underdevelopment, which in fact goes against the sentiments of French people toward this cause, as we see in many surveys.[2] The lack of political decision making is out of step with public opinion. At the legislative, academic, and scientific levels, France is lagging behind. Politicians refuse to hear society's expectations. It's as if they have blinders on.

Power is a perverse and self-absorbed force. From the moment a being possesses it, he or she will have only one goal: to hold onto it, even if it means betraying what established that power in the first place. This is part of the reason why animals are still treated like the fifth wheel. It has been ages since animal protection organizations first requested the creation of a government ministry dedicated to their cause—which would put an end to this scrambling among the Ministries of Ecology, Agriculture, Health, Justice, and Culture—but the desire is not there, the courage nonexistent. The adversaries of animals are too powerful and too connected to political power. France is managing to circumvent European directives on animal protection with exemptions to appease the major agricultural, industrial, medical, and food lobbies.

This is why an animal protection lobby is needed if animals are going to be saved. Groups with influence that can exert pressure must be created. I took part in a sort of "direct lobbying" in 1980, and following my request, Valéry Giscard d'Estaing met with his minister of transportation to put an end to crash tests at a road safety research laboratory that used monkeys and pigs in its experiments. Something similar happened again a few years later when a scandalous affair was reported in the press.

---

2 Eurobaromètre 2016: 94 percent of European citizens think that the protection of the well-being of farm animals is important, 82 percent think that farm animals should be better protected than they are currently, and 89 percent agree that there should be European legislation to guarantee the well-being of animals used for commercial ends: http://www .vetitude.fr/eurobarometre-lattitude- des-europeens-vis-a-vis-du-bien-etre-animal-decryptee/.

An organization that would later be named the Dog Connection had been stealing dogs to feed medical and pharmaceutical laboratories. Right at that moment, I was working on my second *S.O.S.* program dedicated to animal experimentation. The minister of research and technology, Hubert Curien, immediately contacted me to help him present ten measures regulating animal experimentation. Those measures were adopted and included a requirement to trace where laboratory animals were coming from.

My influence on the powers in place was also successful in 1996 with the very humane minister of agriculture, Philippe Vasseur. When he discovered the insufferable agony that horses were undergoing because of caudectomies, he immediately outlawed the practice. Vasseur also developed a legislative project to protect pets in France. The project was supposed to be submitted to the Assemblée Nationale, but Jacques Chirac had the brilliant idea of dissolving it in April 1997.

Unfortunately, apart from the few exceptions cited above, I must admit that the majority of political men only met with me out of curiosity or for the media attention I represented. I remember Michel Crépeau, minister of justice under François Mitterrand, being completely indifferent to my request concerning a ban on vivisection, and Jacques Toubon, garde des Sceaux, was unfazed by the disturbing images of zoophilic practices I showed him.

I'm sometimes nostalgic for those moments when I could still travel and lay my heart at the feet of those decision makers, trying to convince them face to face as I did in 2007 when I met with President Sarkozy to discuss three things: the requirement to stun animals before their slaughter, already mentioned in the previous chapter; the outlawing of importing products of seal hunting; and, last, the creation of a Grenelle Animal Round Table, something that would indeed see the light of day in 2008 with the famous *Animal et Société* meetings, the results of which would be far from our lofty expectations.

During one of these *Animal et Société* meetings, for example, one group had developed points promoting the legal status of animals, and Michel Barnier, then minister of agriculture, was supposed to present the results of their work. He was never able to, however, because the FNSEA put too much pressure on him.[3] The animal protection organizations began to realize that they needed to combine forces, and this is how the Animal Politique collective was formed, bringing together twenty-six animal protection organizations. In 2017, the goal was to put animal issues at the forefront of political debate with a manifesto of thirty proposals that was submitted to the presidential candidates in the hope of obtaining their signatures.[4]

We are defending life, trying to put an end to a system of exploitation, we are arguing for what should come next, and we are developing alternative options. We are defending what is not concrete, what is not quantifiable; we are defending conscience and justice, an achievable utopia.

Just Between Us

What will you remember about me? A naughty dance to the sound of a boisterous mambo? A cry in the silence of a crowded courtroom? What will you remember about this little Parisian woman who became a star by accident, this idealist who decided one day to dedicate the time she had left on Earth to saving animals? The past only takes its meaning from the present, and the present only takes its meaning from the future.

---

3 Fédération nationale des syndicats d'exploitants agricoles (National Federation of Agricultural Holders' Unions).
4 Special thanks to Christophe Marie for these precisions regarding lobbies.

and this will not depend on me. Between image and action, between the passion and the reason, what will remain of Brigitte Bardot in you?

You will probably remember a sulky pout, or perhaps my outrage, that desire to rebel that I've always had, my indignation in the face of what is unacceptable. You will perhaps remember my desire to overturn preconceived ideas and old habits that paralyze the conscience. If you take a path like mine, you'll occasionally make mistakes, you'll often suffer solitude, and you'll always face refusal, without fail. But you'll never accept the reasons that people will give you for the sake of convenience or a lack of courage, and you'll reject conformity. Your goal will be to break down injustice with the only weapon that is worth anything: sincerity.

You'll probably remember the full and rounded shapes of my initials, and perhaps the transparency of my being. Both an asset and an inconvenience, this openness has brought me many setbacks but also many passions. Maybe you'll remember the way I speak without thinking first, the way I allow for my own excesses and take ownership, with conviction, of my inability to adapt to the superfluous, the false, to what is untrue, and my desire for truth.

You'll probably recollect the icon, and perhaps the Animal Fairy. Children have always called me that, and I find it adorable. People have often separated my life before from my life after, my life in cinema from my life in animal protection, the way one opposes light and dark, a life of glory and then one of bitterness. Condemning injustice with harsh words: is that bitterness? To be honest, the only feeling I hold in my heart is what an animal would feel. Because the animal, whether he is wild or domestic, doesn't live in the throes of emotions, in caustic spite or aggressive revenge. On the contrary, he accepts, he puts things together, he forgives, and, very often, he remains faithful. So when I made the animal cause my own, I also embraced the anger that is foreign to them.

You'll probably remember a commercial legend, and perhaps my imprint on a place, my Tropézien refuge, my Madrague, the doors of which will always be open to you and which will forever be a symbol of my love for animals. If you go, you may be able to sense some of the simplicity that has impregnated the walls of my homes.

You will probably remember one or two of my songs, and perhaps a certain enchantment, a word that means so much to me that it breathes itself into my dreams, this attitude of openness and searching, this need for somewhere else and another way, this desire to blend the human and the animal into the same nature, this way of giving in to the pain in order to enjoy the caress. This is the enchantment of life that has kept me away from death, because of my constant seeking out of what is beautiful, true, and essential. In everything, in everyone, and everywhere.

You will probably remember a fictional tale and perhaps a true story, one about a woman who realized one day that she would be making the biggest mistake of her life if she didn't lift the taboo on animal humanity and human animality. Living beings, all living beings, have a common past, present, and future. I want to see an animal history, and I want it to begin today.

Epilogue

Saint Brigitte

On July 23, 2017, for the first time in my life, I thought about giving up my public battle for the animal cause. The reason for this was a profound and intense disgust I felt at the treatment inflicted upon wolves in our region. The French government had decided to satisfy the farmers by authorizing forty additional killings for the current season. Once again, force had prevailed, and once again, the animal was the victim of man's inability to adapt to nature. This decision killed me, especially because it had been agreed to by Minister Nicolas Hulot, in whom I had placed so much faith. It was a resounding blow to animal protection, and I truly believed that it would sound the death knell for my activism. I burned with anger and shame and was consumed in ashes of bitterness. I was certain I was no longer of any use.

Sitting in the middle of my living room, facing the sea and the sailboats dancing in the Bay of Saint-Tropez, I examined my dozens, my *hundreds,* of photos pinned to the walls and lost myself in my memories, in all of those encounters, journeys, victories, and difficulties that had punctuated my life. I thought about the meaning of choice: to choose was to sacrifice, to choose was to be. What had I imagined in 1973? That I could save the world, that my power and my reputation were such that they could move mountains?

Filled with confusion, I left for La Garrigue and sat down at the desk that adjoins my kitchen, the desk where I worked every day, where I relentlessly continued my battle against animal mistreatment. But on July 23, I had no strength left, none. I was feverish, withdrawn, and felt out of place. Supported by my two old crutches, which could hold a lot more than my tired hips, I decided to undertake an ascension I hadn't made in a long time. It took me several long minutes to reach the door to my chapel. Noisily and somewhat carelessly, I sat down inside and waited for the Little Virgin to answer my requests. She knew why I had come; she could see my sorrow. This time I wouldn't ask for anything. She would need to bring me some kind of immediate comfort.

I received only silence in return. Was an alleviation possible? When the taste for fighting leaves us, is there anything to be done?

The fighter was down. I had never felt such helplessness before . . . and I cried; deep groans burst from my body. I hurled my failure and my uselessness on the ground.

And I thought about writing, again and again, about publishing yet another communiqué, tossing another stone into the pond, shouting out to the world that I was leaving, making noise, shining a light on the France who was abandoning her children, her animal citizens, the France who was abandoning her values of justice, liberty, and respect, the France who was abandoning her image as a land of welcome, of refuge for the weakest. But even this desire left me.

When I made the decision to leave cinema, my motivation was clear: I had given the best part of myself, and all I had left to offer was the "less than best." On that July 23, I took stock of those forty-four years of animal activism: I had fought, worn myself out, fed my hopes, and all I had encountered was a lack of courage, sensitivity, and intelligence in the women and men who could have changed things. I had given everything, and I no longer saw how I could intercede again. For decades, I had walked through the doors of presidents, ministers, and members of the European government, and I had always been promised the moon. There had been progress, but none of the great victories I wished for. And each failure was another blow to my weakened body.

This battle gave me strength as much as it destroyed me. Animal protection was never a trivial hobby or a career. I lived it, I dissolved into it. All those years, I was never able to live peacefully if I met a lost dog; I couldn't sleep because I was thinking about a big cat pacing incessantly in an enclosure, and I was incapable of waking up with a spring in my step when I knew that millions of animals had been led to the slaughter that very morning.

These thoughts haunted me. Constantly.

My compassion for the beings without a voice, for the slaves without rights, has been limitless.

Why was my fate so tied to that of animals? Why were they my family, my reason for being and moving forward in my existence?

I am certain that animal protection was a mission I was given, in life and in death, to make heard the pleas of humanity's eternal sacrificial beings.

Until now, my rebellion had kept me on the edge of my seat; it gave me a purpose in my life day after day. But the well was beginning to run dry. My ideals had been swept away by my despair. I no longer recognized myself, and I no longer understood the meaning of my dedication.

Immersed in spirituality, searching for an answer in the quiet of my little chapel, I had lost the desire to resist.

Suddenly, I felt hot, damp tears run down my cheeks; the tears that had left me so long ago were coming back to me like a hope and an opportunity.

I was crying the tears of battle.

And I quickly realized that these providential tears would be the foundation for something else, that they were being shed for the future of animals, for myself, and also for those who would take up the torch after me.

I couldn't abandon them, I couldn't let them see the fighter down.

My despair needed to arouse new hopes.

The battle had to go on: there were other wolves to save, slaughterhouses to abolish, and circuses with wild animals to be banned.

On July 23, I realized that my mission was coming to its end, that soon I would not be a part of these battles, at least not like I was before. This book, these "tears of battle," will therefore be my inheritance. This testimonial text will forever carry on my conviction, my dejection, and my hopes.

Like voices coming from another place, these realizations suddenly impressed themselves upon me. It was July 23, Saint Brigitte's Day. And this was not an accident. Something behind all of this had a meaning. Perhaps when I left a life of artifice in 1973, which to me was what the film industry represented, I had said good-bye to "Bardot." From then on, I had been saying good-bye to "Brigitte."

I measured the extent and the significance of what I had done; I knew that it would make a difference for millions of animal defenders, and that one day the animal would be considered an individual in his own right, that things would change, that the current increases in awareness would be the genesis of an animal revolution.

With my last tear shed, I felt certain that this fierce battle for the respect of life wouldn't go on forever. My heirs are already ready for battle; my battle was continuing on without me, and I had hardly noticed.

On Saint Brigitte's Day, I realized that one day, perhaps not so far off, from wherever I will be, I will feel the breath of life that I fought for my entire existence. An invigorating, powerful, and pioneering breath. An invincible breath, coming from the women and men who will open, once and for all, the gates to this "immense world of dreams and silent griefs" that is animality.[1] My passage on Earth will therefore not have been in vain. And my soul will finally be at peace.

To the women and men who fight against the mistreatment of animals, to their children, and to the future generations: I love you, infinitely and deeply.

My soul is animal.

---

1 Reference to Jules Michelet's very beautiful phrase in *Le Peuple* in 1846: "The animal! Mysterious! Immense world of dreams and silent griefs." Translation from: *Awe for the Tiger, Love for the Lamb: A Chronicle of Sensibility to Animals,* edited by Rod Preece, Routledge, 2002.

Acknowledgments

Bernard d'Ormale
Christophe Marie
Christophe Laury

Appendix I

December 8, 2005

Bonsoir Brigitte,

The letter that started it all . . . it's quite moving to read it today.

With all my affection,
Christophe

65 Boulevard Lannes
Paris 75016
Tel: 504.22.85
February 17, 1977

Dear Franz Weber,

I read in "La Suisse" about the unfortunate result of your marvelous initiative.

I myself have experienced a spectacular failure with the ghastly outcome of what was to be a wonderful undertaking, the Fondation Brigitte Bardot.

We learn in algebra that the product of two negatives is a positive. What I mean is I am with you, my time, my name, my money—I may be able to be of some use to you! The problem of baby seals is particularly important to me. I have the desire to conquer human ignorance and cruelty, only I am weak, too fragile, attacked from every side. With you, your strength, your courage, I have the sense that we might if not win, then at least make some serious progress.

I am at your disposal. I so want to be useful to this cause.

Brigitte Bardot

Appendix II

The European Union and the Animal Condition . . . France Is Lagging Behind!

SPECIAL CASES

In Belgium, there are three ministers assigned to "animal well-being" (not connected to the Ministry of Agriculture and Environment). In the Netherlands, an animal police force exists with an emergency number for animal abuse and mistreatment. This police force is trained to enforce the laws protecting pets, farm animals, and wild animals. This brigade is composed of 125 uniformed policemen. In Sweden, Stockholm also has an animal police, and a specialized police unit was also created in Norway (outside the European Union).

RITUAL SLAUGHTER

During a slaughter, the general rule according to EU regulation requires stunning the animal, but member states are able to circumvent this in the case of a ritual slaughter, which is what happens in France. Numerous countries nevertheless prohibit the slaughter of animals without prior stunning, including Austria, Belgium (Wallonia in June 2018 and Flanders in September 2019), Denmark, Estonia, Finland, Greece, Luxembourg, the Netherlands, Sweden, and other countries outside the EU like Iceland and Switzerland.

FORCE-FEEDING

According to the 95/58/CE directive, force-feeding is illegal because the text stipulates that "no animal should be fed or watered in such a way that it results in unnecessary suffering or injury" (article 14). France remains the number one producer of foie gras worldwide with the practice of force-feeding banned in Germany, Austria, Denmark, Finland, Ireland, Italy, Luxembourg, the Netherlands, Poland, the Czech Republic, the United Kingdom, and Sweden.

HUNTING

France is the only European country where a person can hunt seven days a week, where cruel practices like *déterrage* (hunting underground) or foxhunting are permitted even though they are forbidden elsewhere. Foxhunting has been outlawed in Germany since 1952, in the United Kingdom since 2004, and in Belgium since 1995.

The badger, a victim of *déterrage* in France, is a protected species in England, Belgium, Denmark, Spain, Greece, Hungary, Italy, Luxembourg, the Netherlands, and Portugal.

CAPTIVITY

Within the EU, eleven countries do not have a dolphinarium: Austria, Cyprus (banned since 1997), the Czech Republic, Estonia, Hungary (banned since 2002), Latvia, Luxembourg, Poland, Ireland, Slovakia, and Great Britain (not illegal but with strict standards that led to the closing of all dolphinariums in the nineties).

Currently, twenty-one member states have adopted restrictions on the use of wild animals in circuses, among which thirteen have outlawed it completely: Austria, Belgium, Bulgaria, Croatia, Cyprus, Greece, Ireland, Italy, Latvia, Malta, the Netherlands, Romania, and Slovenia.

ANIMAL EXPERIMENTATION

The six countries financing alternative methods the most are Germany, Austria, Belgium, Finland, the United Kingdom, and Sweden.

In the Netherlands and Italy, students (and, in Italy, physicians, researchers, and technicians, as well) have the right to conscientious objection, which allows them to follow a curriculum without the use of an animal component.

FUR

European fur farms account for 70 percent of worldwide mink fur production and 63 percent of fox fur production.

In Germany, breeding animals for fur is outlawed in several Länder states. In England, the ban has been national since January 1, 2003, for ethical reasons. In Austria, six out of nine federal states have banned the breeding of animals for fur, and in the three others, there is such strict regulation—in particular concerning the availability of bathing water—that breeding has become no longer economically viable. In Belgium, only Flanders registers breeders, and the Walloon government has approved a ban on breeding animals "uniquely and principally" for fur. Breeding animals for fur is outlawed in Bulgaria and in Croatia, and in Denmark (principal producer of mink), the breeding of foxes will be outlawed in 2024. In Italy, the last fox breeding farm was closed in 1997.

For mink, the banning of cages—in favor of open-air enclosures with branches and burrows as well as a four-square-yard pool twenty inches in depth—put an end to breeding because it became economically unprofitable. In the Netherlands, the breeding, of chinchillas and foxes for fur is forbidden. The third-largest producer of mink fur, the Netherlands, has banned mink breeding since the end of 2012 (an extension was granted until 2024). And final, Slovenia has outlawed breeding animals for their fur.

It should be noted that in the European Union, the importation and trading of domestic dog and cat skins and all products derived from seals (and other pinnipeds) is outlawed.

On all of these matters of animal protection, France has no special provisions of any kind and for this reason is lagging behind other member states.

Document prepared by Christophe Marie
Director of the Office of Animal Protection
Fondation Brigitte Bardot

Appendix III

"Hunting"
Song written by Jean-Max Rivière for Brigitte Bardot

Benjamin Bunny, my friend from school
Where have you been since the hunt
That spilled so much blood?
Cruel hunter, you are mean
Igor, my friend the boar
Are you still in your bush
Or were you killed?
Hunter, how merciless you are

Chorus:
Hide yourselves away, forest friends
The hunter is coming, I am his dog
I will warn you, forest friends
When I bark, the hunter is coming

Yvette, my partridge friend
Have you lost Pierre the pheasant?
You made a lovely couple
Two of the most charming lovebirds
Arthur the elk looked so dashing
As he pranced through the forest
Menacing woodsmen,
What have you done with him?

(Chorus)

Antoine, the wild duck
With his hard beak and soft plumage
You had seen so much of the countryside
Did they shoot you down?
Weasel friends, fox friends
Little pigeons and squirrels,
Where will I see you again?
The forest is now just a coffin

(Chorus)

God, let the woods always be filled
With animal friends
Beware of men who kill
They do not know how to stop